T0170885

what happened to my happily ever after?

THE RADICAL APPROACH TO REVITALIZE YOUR MARRIAGE OR DIVORCE WITH LOVE

BELINDA N. ZYLBERMAN JD, MA

what happened to my happily ever after?
THE RADICAL APPROACH TO REVITALIZE YOUR MARRIAGE OR DIVORCE WITH LOVE

Difference Press, Washington, D.C., USA
Copyright © Belinda N. Zylberman, 2020

ISBN: 978-1-68309-257-5

Cover Design: Jennifer Stimson
Editor: Todd Hunter
Author's photo courtesy of Gillian Hunter

DIFFERENCE
PRESS

For Siena,
who opened my heart to the practice of
unconditional loving.

TABLE OF CONTENTS

FOREWORD

*In theory, there is no difference between
theory and practice. In practice, there is.
- BENJAMIN BREWSTER
The Yale Literary Magazine, February 1882*

This author is one those interesting people you can't really describe with a brief introduction – she doesn't fit any one box or any simple set of labels. I have known her for going on 20 years and still struggle to find that one "woke" word that is the essence of who she is and the work she does. Some part of her can be explained by the story of her upbringing, which will captivate you with accounts of Holocaust survivors, Upstate NY small-town USA, ascetic Catholics, war torn countries, world travel, fencing, fighting, torture, revenge, giants, monsters, chases, escapes, true love, miracles... and so much more.[1] Another part could be explained by her education and life's work – her resume could run for pages and still not cover the wide variety of things she's studied and done. But the aspect of her that I most struggle to bring to life for you, as an engineer and a businessman, is that intangible trait that I can only call "ancient wisdom." It's not derived from any one school of spirituality, one philosophy, one ethnicity, or one period of time, but many. With that wisdom, she can pierce through the clutter of a complex conflict and see the essence of it. Then, by stating a sometimes-uncomfortable truth, or asking a poignant question, she will illuminate the path out and a way forward. When she figures out what the conflict is all about, you can see in her eyes that little inner excitement, like that of a six-year-old who has just figured out how some complex contraption actually works, with just a few simple pulleys and levers, no magic required.

With this book, the author carefully explores her innate sense of conflict, and then breaks it down into simple steps that the rest of us regular Earthlings can understand and follow. She calls it

---

1   The part starting from "fencing" on is graciously borrowed from the movie *Princess Bride*, but some of those events show up in Belinda's life story too.

"The P-R-A-C-T-I-C-E." Step by step, starting with P for "Pause" and ending with (I won't spoil the ending), the mystery is gone, the bare facts are on the table, and the way forward is clear. If "The P-R-A-C-T-I-C-E" existed in 1982, we would have never had that hit from *The Clash* - "Should I Stay or Should I Go" – it would have been obvious to them what to do, avoiding both the trouble and the double. What's more, once the mystery and darkness of conflict is reduced to a few simple and some-time brutally honest facts, it takes the fear out of anticipating the next conflict and encourages us to embrace it when it inevitably comes about. It is exactly this newly learned skill of applying *courage* around conflict that is the most important takeaway from the book. The courage to face, and if necessary, initiate conflict without resorting to distraction, emotions, and ugliness.

I suppose, in closing, I should unveil how it is that I know so much about the author and her work. You will hear about me in the book by direct reference, but parts of me can also be found among the many conflict examples the author provides throughout. I am her ex-husband, and during our near 20-year long relationship as part-ners, spouses, and co-parents, I've lived in real life what she teaches in this book. Today, both remarried, parenting and co-parenting, we are a "blended family squared," navigating the delights and the struggles that being such a family presents. And while we certainly have not always followed her methodology in real time, we've always come around to the basics she teaches here. Not just in theory, but in practice.

Dr. Elvir Causevic
San Francisco, California 2019

INTRODUCTION

We came into this world made of love. We will exit this world having known love. Most of our life in between, we are seeking, resisting, suffering, and longing for love. We want love, but in its place, more often we experience conflict. When we do receive love, even though our hearts sing, our minds continue to remind us that conflict is just around the corner, so better get love while it's still there.

Most of us perceive conflict as an absence of love. We are wired to seek love and avoid conflict. But there's only one problem: in the pursuit of love we discover that conflict is inevitable, and in the state of conflict, it is the hardest place for us to access the love we seek. We find ourselves once again stuck in a dilemma: conflict or love.

Conflict magnifies the vulnerability of feeling separate and alone right when we need love and connection the most. When we're in conflict, we are unconsciously asking for affirmation of our significance and belonging.

When I listen to couples in their initial sessions, they're not talking about love. They're expressing anger, disappointment, judgment, pain, suffering, hatred, and betrayal. They reflect on the naivety in their thinking when years or decades earlier they believed "I do" was enough to get them their happily ever after. They remember that once upon a time there was a grand plan, or at least the inklings of a grand plan, but somewhere along the line, it was forgotten or pushed to the side while "real life" took over. Or, some acknowledge that there never was a plan.

All in the pursuit of love.

But what if the presence of conflict did not equate to an absence of love? What if conflict was not intrinsically bad?

In the following pages, I'll invite you to consider the significant role conflict plays in your most important relationship. By considering another point of view, you may no longer run from, resist, or judge conflict, and may even come to embrace it and let it be. In so doing, you are likely to reach an understanding that conflict is not the absence of love, but a quintessential part of coming into the most desired state of human love – unconditional love. Consider the places inside us where we are most conflicted, as they reveal a rare insight. Consider that conflict and the presence of strong emotions tell us that something matters. Whatever we fear, resist, fight against, or judge, matters, including:

The seeking of the love.

Unconditional love.

Self-love.

I propose that conflict is just one step in a journey of seeking that love. If you decide to join me in this exploration, perhaps you'll come to understand the significance of conflict in your life.

The question is, are you willing to take that risk? Are you willing to challenge your preconceived notions? Are you willing to let go of what you think you know, in order to discover what you didn't know? Can you fathom that an even greater possibility exists? If so, keep reading and join me on this path of seeking love, and understanding conflict....

CHAPTER 1

I Can't Do This Anymore

"The cave you fear to enter holds the treasure you seek."
– JOSEPH CAMPBELL

You believed that it was enough to love him; that it was enough to believe in love. It was enough to marry him, speak those vows, and trust that each of you were being truthful. That it was enough to have some shared dreams, even if you had no idea how you would manifest them.

You believed it was enough to say to yourself, "I'm not going to do it like my parents" – or maybe the opposite, that you would live like your parents because they're still together....

You believed you could make it work. Maybe you told yourself it was more your fault than his. If only you could be happy. If only you could accept life as it was. If only it was enough.

But it wasn't, and it isn't, and it's costing you. It's costing you your joy. It's costing you your sanity. It's costing you valuable time that you know you can never get back.

Even worse, it's costing you your dignity. Living this life half-in and half-out – with one foot always out the door. You're not happy, you're not grounded, and you're not you.

But, you don't know if leaving is the right answer. You've seen so many others divorce, and while they might seem happier at first, you wonder, *are* they really happier? Then you hear about their new relationship, but when you listen closely, you can sense the same rumblings. Different man, same experience. Or, single and still unhappy. Or even worse, single and searching for such an "evolved" man that no one is ever good enough.

Some of you might think, "My parents are still together, they make it work. Shouldn't that be good enough?" But when you're really honest, you suspect they aren't living their full lives either, and you wonder, "Was staying really the right answer for them?"

Then there are your children, your extended family, your friends, your colleagues, and your community. What will they think? How will you live amongst them? How might leaving change everything?

Perhaps most of all, living this way has been costing you your dreams. You may not even remember them anymore. Whether from childhood or young adulthood, those thoughts and feelings pulled you toward something – the future you dreamed of having with that perfect person. You thought this relationship would help you get there, that this relationship was *the way* there. That he was with you on the path to those very dreams. So what happened? Because you're not there, you're here. And maybe you barely even remember where "there" was supposed to be.

Perhaps you haven't let yourself dream in a long time simply because it's too painful.

You've been in this place a long time, dear reader, and you can't stay here anymore. Even though every fiber in your being wants to stay – you feel afraid to stay, and afraid to go. It's the fear of the possible consequences, the potential hurt, the unaddressed misunderstandings, and the journey into or away from the sadness that's kept you here for too long.

But now what? You know you're here, unhappy, frustrated, tired, and uninspired. You have an idea about how you got here, but you really don't know what to do next. Leave your spouse and start over? Stay and try to make it work? Try harder, try one more thing? Focus more on you than him? Make him go to therapy?

You are so full of love to give – if only it could be easier. If only you could trust it would be reciprocated. If only you knew it was desired. You have so much love that it makes you hurt. It's why you've fought so hard on your journey that got you here, because of the love you have to give and the love you seek.

I don't believe it would hurt this much if it didn't matter. It matters that you are loved and that you can feel free to love. It matters that you live your truth. It matters that your kids have every opportunity in love and in life. And even though you may not feel the desire to direct these feelings toward your spouse at this moment (quite the contrary perhaps), I believe you do desire that he lives up to his greatest self and deserves to experience the love he has to give and wants to receive.

You've been on the verge of leaving. You love each other, but it's not enough. You feel stifled, held back, misunderstood, and unheard. You thought you knew each other, but there are days you wake up next to a stranger. You look in the mirror and you, yourself, might feel like the stranger.

You're not exactly sure when it happened. It was subtle, over time. It could've been before children, before the house, or before the wedding. You felt that tingling. But now you're years in and deeply committed. You wonder why you didn't go then. But what did you have to go on? A few feelings? A dumb fight or an act of betrayal that you thought for sure was a one-time thing? So, you believed him, he believed you, you told yourself a story you could live with, and you went on. For a while, it was lovely. Your relationship kept its promises. You felt happy. Until you didn't.

The fighting, mistrust, misunderstandings, and silence replaced the lovemaking and happier times. You thought, "Here I am again." You thought, "We can get through this." You lived this scene so many times. The back and forth. The life inside your home was not the life you were living when people saw you pick up your children from school or socialize at a dinner party. A year went by, and then another, and another. You kept telling yourself that it was good enough, but the little voice inside contradicted you. While you did hear this voice, you ignored it. What else could you do? You weren't going to leave. Too much invested. Too much time, love, energy, and money. Too many people to consider. So, you made them more important than yourself, and you justified this because that's what a good mother, daughter, woman, wife, sister, friend does.

Until she can't do it anymore.

The good news is that you don't have to live this way anymore. There is another possibility available if you're willing to open your mind, open your heart, and explore this path. Where you will end up, we do not yet know. But now is not the time to concern yourself with the outcome. Allow yourself to take it one step at a time.

Dear reader, I have been where you are now, and I promise you there is a light at the end of this tunnel. To get there, however, you must first walk through the darkness.

While it's scary and uncertain, I believe you are in the perfect place, and it's the perfect time to walk this path. While you don't yet know the right answer for your marriage – whether you should stay and recommit – or leave and let it go – you are asking questions and you have pledged to take the steps necessary to make the best choice for you. Soon, dear reader, your answers will come.

In the quest for happiness will you be happier without your husband? Can you handle loneliness? Will you find a new loving partner? You think yes, I'll stay, and the next moment you want out. You no longer recall the dreams of your younger, excited self. Your parents are still together but are they truly happy? Should you stay for the kids? For the security? You wanted to leave years ago but you pushed those thoughts down. Concentrating now on what you want will help. In your conflicted state, now is the time to go deeper into your own dreams and perceptions of your union to become clear on your own decisions.

There is a way out: considering yourself and exploring your own feelings without making a move. Contemplating what your own heart desires and what your freedom would feel like. Finding a way to look at your spouse differently, even lovingly. Embracing conflict. Right now, there can be freedom in your mind, your heart and your life, even if you're still there in the home with your spouse. Allowing for guidance will alter your current reality. Your consciousness will be enlivened and awakened to make the difficult choices. Have you ever made conscious choices or have they been mostly impulsive or unconscious? Was life generally about someone else's needs? What does happiness even look like?

First, we will start with *you*.

CHAPTER 2

My Dissatisfying Life as a Subtle Victim

"The truth will set you free, but first it will piss you off."
– JOE KLAAS

"To love oneself is the beginning of a lifelong romance."
– OSCAR WILDE

I grew up in a fundamentally unhappy house, the daughter of two unhappy people who could never quite put their finger on the cause of their unhappiness.

There were moments, though, when a rapturous laughter could be heard within the walls of our home. My father was a Holocaust survivor, and in the Jewish culture, humor was often used as a strategy to navigate the complexity of living in the moment while grappling with thousands of years of persecution. Humor saved us.

But these moments were always short-lived. As I developed into a teenager, my unhappiness revolved around my body, hormonal fluctuations, boyfriends (lack thereof), broken friendships, and an overall negative disposition. It never occurred to my parents (or me) that my unhappiness could have been a result of an environment that focused on pain, struggle, and conflict, almost to the point of identifying proudly – righteously, even – with these experiences.

As a child, I observed those closest to me as unwilling participants in the events of their lives. I was conditioned to believe that "life happens to you" and there's not much you can do about it.

In June 1986, when my mother turned to my sister and me from the driver's seat of her station wagon to say she was leaving my father, the cause of her unhappiness was revealed. To pursue happiness, she needed to leave my father.

The following year, I left for college and visited my parents infrequently, temporarily concluding that they, in fact, were the cause of my unhappiness. A year later, my conclusion was affirmed when three months into my sophomore year, at home for Thanksgiving, my father revealed he had been diagnosed with terminal lung cancer. It was as if I too, had been given a sentence.

Although I loved him, my desperate and often depressed mood, defined our relationship and my obligatory visits home over the next three years. My father's illness chained me on my quest for freedom and belonging. I didn't know meshing my state of mind with his was not an obligatory act of love, nor was it helping him or helping me. I could hear laughter in the dorm, be at parties, see friends in relationships, but it was difficult for me to partake in the merriment with his death hanging over my head.

I blamed my unhappiness on both of my parents as I judged their individual struggles, and judged the victimizing stance by which I believed I was raised. I resented them for it, as I myself struggled and lived as a victim.

When I graduated college, I returned home to live with my father, in essence, to wait for him to die.

When he did, after the funeral and the frenetic disposal of most of the household contents (with my mother in Belgium in a new relationship and my sister back at university), I was left without my bag of excuses for my unhappiness, a bag I had been carrying around as long as I could remember. I perceived an awkward but palpable feeling of freedom (I share more about my childhood and family experiences in later chapters).

I recognized for a brief moment, in my new-found independence, that I could choose my path. Either shift my life toward self-sufficiency and self-actualization or continue making someone else responsible for my happiness. The idea of the first choice was so appealing. However, the second choice was the only one I knew. I chose the second.

I travelled, got a job at a law firm, and headed into law school thinking I might find my happiness there (huh?). Instead, I found myself in utter terror. Single, alone in New York City, six months from graduating – and feeling pressure to have my life figured out (or at least, how I was going to pay for my life), I did the only "reasonable" thing a young woman does in these situations. I got married.

At that time, I truly believed that if my parents' bad relationship was responsible for their unhappiness, then a good relationship could be responsible for my happiness, right?

Consequently, I chose a man who I thought chose me. I believed that choosing each other would make us happy. While some friends warned me that I was making a poor decision, the rose-colored glasses I was wearing led me to believe he was indeed the answer to my happiness.

As you might imagine, the illusion that the simple act of marrying someone would bring me love, quickly faded. I felt deeply frustrated on a daily basis as I watched him make life choices around family, money, career, and his mental and physical health that felt out of sync with my values. Within months of marrying him, I'd questioned my choices. But I had made a commitment, and I believed I could make it work because I had a dream.

I dreamed of the romantic love affair that could seasonally renew. I detested the notion that a relationship had its "high" in the first months/ years, assisted by elevated hormones and pheromones, only later to be reduced to something pleasant and boring. I wanted to feel in love with life! I wanted to co-create with a man. I wanted a partner. I wanted someone I could be my best with... and my worst. I truly desired "until death do us part," determined to do it differently than my parents.

I was failing miserably, caught between two bad choices.

The first choice was to stay and live out my life in frustration and disappointment, out of alignment with my values, betraying myself time and time again. The second choice was to leave, admit defeat, and succumb to the reality that my friends and family had been right. Worst of all, I would have to accept blame for my semi-conscious and ill-informed choices, and retreat to being alone and afraid again.

The deeper dilemma I was frightened to consider was that if my experience of love depended on me, it would mean contradicting everything I had observed and integrated about relationship, conflict, marriage, and the pursuit of happiness. This journey, a third choice, would require me to rely on myself and take full responsibility for my happiness.

I wasn't ready. I had no idea what that would look like. What does a woman in this situation do? She gets divorced, quickly moves into her next relationship, and gets married again.

But this time, it was with a soulmate! Really, I have no doubt that this man was my soulmate. I was in love with him before I even met him. I fell in love with his children, ages three and five at the time. I was convinced that I had made a better choice this time. Our early years together were mostly magical as I experienced elements of a true partnership that lifted me up to accomplish some great things: we travelled, lived and worked abroad, created businesses together, bore a child, and loved deeply.

Then, it happened again.

At 39 I was facing the end of a second marriage. Overnight, I became a single parent to a toddler, an "ex" stepparent to two stepdaughters, and I was alone, again. As the most inspiring and challenging relationship of my life ended, I could no longer avoid the most difficult and unaddressed relationship of my life, my relationship with myself.

I went home, not back to my childhood home in upstate New York (which was sold many years earlier), but rather to Brussels, Belgium, to be near my mother and sister, make peace with my childhood, and make sense of my adulthood.

I was again faced with the third choice from way back when. This time I knew the only choice was to rely on and begin a relationship with myself, to discover the path to the love within me. In so doing, I began to recognize that this was my sole (soul) responsibility, because even the "soul-mate magic love" I experienced with my second husband could not get that job done.

The next three years in Belgium looked like this: voraciously reading, ugly and cathartic crying, hours lying on the couch staring into space, and acquiring a job working for a multinational company that felt like my first "grown up" job only to leave ten months later (in what my Belgian doctor would diagnose as "burnout"). I sampled individual therapy, dove into group therapy, and engaged in family dinners, family fights, and binge-watching the American TV I could find on the internet like "Desperate Housewives" and "Sex in the City" (a girl can dream, right?). Bread and cheese became my staple foods. I followed a regular yoga practice which took me to three life-changing weeks in India. And when I thought I was ready, I went on two dates via the internet, and made an awkward attempt at a new relationship that lasted a whole two-weeks.

Breathe. Pause. Listen. These were the most difficult years of my life. Despite the flurry of work and parenting duties, some deeply formed friendships, and my committed pursuit, I was mostly alone. The solitude was often excruciating. For the first time in my life, I was face-to-face with myself. I didn't know what to do, how to be, or who I was. Though there were moments of joy through the tears, it was a time mostly filled with tears.

Committed to cracking my own code, understanding myself, and walking through the darkness I could no longer avoid, I eventually entered the light. Once there, I experienced something quite profound.

I realized that I had learned how to be with the heartaches, the disappointments, and the feelings of failure. I came to understand that moving beyond identifying with all the pain, turmoil, and conflict (as I had learned from my parents) meant there was space to accept all of what life presented me: love and heartbreak, successes and failures, and trial and error. I rejoiced in the idea that I was able to find my way to love when I embraced all of it.

Up until that moment, I had lived my life with the misunderstanding that a "good" life was one without conflict, without hardship, and without failure. It sounded silly to say aloud, but I had lived a divided life, separating "good" experiences from "bad" ones, "failures" from "successes." I was conditioned to honor only select moments; highlights to be celebrated at the expense of a great deal of life lived. A life lived in trial and error. Indeed, a whole lot of error.

I started to understand a new reality, bridging the gap between how marriage and relationship were sold to me and how love in its greatest form could be experienced.

Most profound was the recognition that the key factor preventing me from reaching love was my resistance to all that I had judged as wrong and bad. That the integration of all my experiences would bring me into wholeness, not a soulmate, a partner, my parents, my sister, or even my daughter. It was embracing the entirety of my life: choices, thoughts, traumas, and upbringing. This embrace, not the embrace of a lover, led me back home, to myself, to love.

Then, and only then, could I receive the unconditional passionate love relationship I had been longing to create.

Through all of the conflict, change, and transition that I experienced, I discovered what I longed for even more than love – my purpose. To know why I was here and what I was supposed to do with this life. I learned to stop, pause, and listen; to dig deep, reflect, accept, and embrace; to ask questions, practice non-judgment, consider, integrate, and practice; to forgive myself and others. This was my purpose. My life (my conflicts) was showing me my purpose all along. My experiences, wisdom – all that I did not know I did not know, and all that I knew that I did not know, was showing me my purpose. I began to live from that place, from a place of knowing and not knowing. A place of inquiry. A place of curiosity. A place of being unwilling to accept status quo, because no one (especially not me) was satisfied there.

In professional practice, as a mediator and relationship coach, I turned my focus on the relationships of others. With humor, love, acceptance, and understanding, I could relate to everyone who walked through my door. I could relate to everyone I met. I began to see that we're not all that different. In fact, quite the opposite. Couple by couple by couple, I saw the same patterns and the same suffering. The stories were different, but the suffering was the same: the same strategies and the same desire to avoid facing conflict. My personal and professional practice illuminated a path of inquiry:

Am I willing to ask questions?

Am I willing to consider another point of view?

Am I choosing judgment or love?

Am I willing to pause?

Am I willing to listen?

Am I willing to risk it all – the status quo and whatever attachments I had up until now – for a magnificent life?

Do I really want this life?

What do I want?

More and more clients started coming to me not wanting to divorce or separate. Rather, they desired relief from the struggle and discomfort by understanding what they lived. Together, we were creating new possibilities and a third choice.

To divorce or not to divorce was simply not the question.

To come to know and love one's self, know one's desires, explore the deeper questions of purpose and conditioning and the lessons to be learned – these became the questions and the practice. We were discovering the correct path for each of us. On this path, the more accurate question is, "Will being in relationship with my spouse continue to support me on my true path?"

The seeking, suffering and longing my clients experienced in their relationships, that I myself had experienced in two marriages, was getting us all nowhere. To discover our answers it would require pausing, curiosity, and inquiry. To our shared delight, when we listened, we heard the answers within.

With that, let our work begin.

Like many young women, I took in the attitudes, environment and depressed feelings emanating from my parents: my dad a Holocaust survivor and my suffering mother, longing for escape. College was often excruciating and committed relationship impossible with my frame of mind, while classmates paired up and got married. Graduating from law school was daunting, and figuring out what would come after even more so. When life becomes what just "happens" to people and this belief is passed down, it obliterates the individual's choice. I broke free when I stopped judging myself and resisting life's ups and downs. I could learn to love myself when I realized that all of my painful experiences led me to discover my purpose. If I knew how to love myself, I could learn how to be in loving partnership with a man. And I shared all of these insights with anyone who would listen, eventually sharing them with my clients.

CHAPTER 3

The P-R-A-C-T-I-C-E

"All adventures, especially into new territory, are scary."
– SALLY RIDE, Astronaut

In creating The P-R-A-C-T-I-C-E, readers are privy to the insights and methods of the work my clients undergo. My mediation and coaching practice takes clients from judging and feeling stuck, to being able to be with **what is**. This includes embracing it all: from fear of letting go of a marriage to fear of embracing personal freedom.

When I hung up the phone on July 4, 2008, it was perhaps one of the darkest moments of my life. It signified the end of my second marriage, a truth made only somewhat bearable by the sweet breathing sounds of my 22 month-old daughter sleeping beside me. The friends I was vacationing with were waiting down the hall with beers, open arms, and an invitation for a conversation about my future.

That conversation was the beginning of what would become, "The P-R-A-C-T-I-C-E." In the following chapters, you will be led through an inquiry and be challenged to consider many questions, undertake some soul searching, and pull off some deep diving.

In Chapter 4, I explore the practice of *pausing*. We live in a time where action is rewarded and reaction is the norm. But this is a cycle that limits us in relationships and prevents us from understanding why we keep experiencing the same thing. In this chapter, we will pause, consider how you got here, and discover what's getting in the way of your happiness.

In Chapter 5, I share the practice of *reflecting* and *receiving*. One of my favorite quotes reminds me that it's through reflection, not simply experience, that we come to understand and quantify what we've been through. Only then can we receive the lessons and wisdom therein.

In Chapter 6, I guide you through the practice of *accepting* and *acknowledging*. Here, I discuss the power of moving beyond "coming to terms with your past" – the good, the bad and the ugly

– to coming to love and embrace your past. The practice of acknowledgment and acceptance takes us one step closer to discovering our happiness and our truth.

In Chapter 7, I present the practice of *curiosity*. Curiosity is a forgotten and disowned state of mind we've been conditioned to believe exists only amongst the young. I challenge this idea and encourage you to consider how practicing a curious mindset rather than judging, supports you in moving through your conflicts and choosing life choices that are most aligned with you.

In Chapter 8, I lovingly take you down the rabbit hole of *trust* and *truth-telling*. One of the most difficult internal conflicts many of us face is to tell the truth especially when we believe it will hurt someone or hurt ourselves. In this chapter, I explore how avoiding telling our truth is doing us and the ones we love a disservice. If we truly want to trust and be trusted, it begins with telling the truth and having the courage to live out the consequences.

In Chapter 9, I explore the practice of *initiation*. While our childhoods provided us with an array of wounds and conflicts, it is the pain of our first heartbreak that holds a unique place in our personal story. In this chapter we'll contemplate that bittersweet entry into adulthood and the stories we began to tell ourselves that limited us in who and how we would love.

In Chapter 10, I present the practice of *choice*. At this point in your journey, it will be your time to choose. You may be ready to take the next step in your relationship. Or, "choosing" may look more like a new way of life as you continue the inquiry of whether to stay or go. The practice of choice focuses on getting to a state of neutrality where true choice lies.

In Chapter 11, I invite you to consider the practice of *exploration*. Here, I challenge you to consider a completely different way of looking at your most difficult relationship. With newly acquired skills of observation, non-judgment and listening, you may explore new ways of being in all of your relationships.

In Chapter 12, we'll bring all the steps together in the integration phase. Integration = practice + reflection + time.

"The P-R-A-C-T-I-C-E" works best when you make it your own by adapting it to your way of walking through the world. Choose what feels correct for you. I stress the idea of choice here because, at the end of this book, it is my goal to support you in arriving at your own truth so that you can make your "happily ever after" choice.

You'll see that there are many exercises described in each chapter – supplemental practices that support the theme of the chapter. I've designed my personal and business practice around these exercises, and I strongly encourage you to take the time to work with them as you read the book. You can read through the book and then come back to the exercises, or read chapter-by-chapter doing the exercises as you go. Trust that you will know the best way for yourself, and, please do the exercises. In my experience, while "aha" moments can shift one's life perspective (and my wish for you is that you have many "aha" moments along the way), implementing practices to assist us in deeply integrating new patterns paves the way for more awareness to bloom. If your goal is to deepen your relationship with yourself and others, then there is no better way than to give yourself the time and consideration to make it so. So, please, do the exercises!

Wherever you are in your journey, I invite you now to bring forward those uncomfortable conflicts, for they are welcome here. Together, let's get underneath the shame, blame, confusion, and hurt, to touch your deepest knowing and reveal your path for foraging ahead.

Most of all, please be gentle with yourself. It's not an accident that these steps are called "The P-R-A-C-T-I-C-E." I cannot stress this enough. Many of us have spent a lifetime in self-judgment, comparison with others, and self-doubt. If I tell you that you are in the exact right place at this very moment, you may choose to believe me or not. Either way is ok. Please believe there's no perfect way and there's no right way. The way that got you to this moment is simply your way. Be gentle with yourself so you may receive the gift of understanding, and with love and intention, design your way to an inspired and love-filled life.

CHAPTER 4

What Happened to Happily Ever After?

"I would like to beg you dear Sir, as well as I can, to have patience with everything unresolved in your heart and to try to love the questions themselves as if they were locked rooms or books written in a very foreign language. Don't search for the answers, which could not be given to you now, because you would not be able to live them. And the point is to live everything. Live the questions now. Perhaps then someday far in the future, you will gradually, without even noticing it, live your way into the answer."
– RAINER MARIA RILKE 'Letters to a young Poet' 1903

"We learn the ropes of life by untying its knots."
– JEAN TOOMER

When we're in relationship turmoil, the "Pause" is what helps us feel our feelings deeply and gain new perspectives. Take them in slowly as fresh questions arrive. Respect all the questions, taking your time with the conclusions. Believe it or not, the conflict you're experiencing is your starting point.

STEP 1: PAUSE

Where am I? Who am I? What does that even mean? Why do I hurt all over? How did I get here? What did I do to deserve this? Someone help me understand how I got here.

Pause.

Pause.

Pause.

Pause.

Pause.

It started as a dream. A dream come true. You thought you did everything right. You were a good person. You were kind. You loved a man and he hurt you. He hurt you to your soul. He destroyed the dream. Was it just your dream? Were you alone in dreaming about a life that you would live together? Were you kidding yourself? Were you making it up all along?

Pause. Begin by pausing and letting in that which you have denied up until now.

I know it hurts. It hurts, and all you want to do is run.

Be here. Be here now. That which you have been seeking only exists here in the now, in this moment. Your pain – how you got here – has been in great part due to running away and avoiding the feelings, avoiding being with yourself. Can you see that?

Pause. Simple, and yet perhaps the most difficult thing to do as a human being.

Pause.

The answers will come in time.

So, how did you get here? How did so much conflict replace so much love? Was it even love? Or was it just a great set of feelings?

These are the questions I came to when I was at the end of my rope. When clients arrive at my door, they are asking the same questions. The tendency is to blame the other, to shove all that pain and responsibility on someone else. The truth is, we're blaming ourselves more than anyone.

Blaming ourselves for not seeing it sooner. Blaming ourselves for believing in something bigger and feeling stupid when it didn't work out to plan.

How did I get here? How did you get here? Where is here?

Conflict is an opening.

LAURA AND THOMAS

When Laura reached out to me, she was at the end of her rope. The holidays were approaching, and it was years since she and her husband were in a good place. She was anxious to get the ball rolling and move towards divorce, even though she struggled with the idea of the finality of it all. It would take them four months before he was ready to begin the process. What unfolded from there was quite unexpected. After a few months of thoughtful conversation, deep listening, and the reframing of their life journey together, they came to understand the value of the pause. With their willingness to slow down and understand how they had gotten here, they were able to create a new possibility for the future. Releasing the outcome and allowing for the pause, they were able to consider what staying together meant as well as leaving, and choose for themselves the best course of action.

Pause. Welcome, dear friend, dear loved one who has suffered and made others suffer by not knowing what you did not know. It's all been perfect in an imperfect kind of way. I know you're saying, "It sure doesn't feel perfect," and yet, perfection it is. It's time to start considering everything that's happened until now. All of it: the good, the bad, and the ugly. There has been good and there has been bad, and depending on what point in time you stand, you will see it one way or another. It's time to stop judging and start asking questions. Start examining your life through different eyes, different measurements, and different questions.

Up until now, you've been so busy judging your life. Have you ever been present enough to live it? I do not judge you here. I simply ask you the question. What percentage of your time do you spend judging and analyzing your life, as opposed to simply being with what is?

We cannot love and judge at the same time.

Pause. Pause. Pause.

Don't worry. If you find that it's a pretty high percentage, it's the perfect time to start shifting that.

You are here because you've been spending so much of your life judging your life and not living it.

The pause. Why have you avoided the pause? Because it's uncomfortable when you have been conditioned to judge, assess, and compare your life to others. You were conditioned to believe it's never been good enough. Your results are here to prove that because even in this moment – especially in this moment – you are probably judging your life. It's in part the reason why you picked up this book and why you're asking these questions. Your life wasn't good enough. You were unhappy. He made you unhappy. All you want is to feel good again.

What you may not realize is that your judgment of him and of your unhappiness, has been getting in your way of a happy life. Comparing your life to a dream you once had or what you perceive others have achieved, is getting in your way of a happy life. Your inability to sit with your uncomfortable feelings, believing that they are the issue, is getting in your way of a happy life. Insisting that your husband is the issue, is getting in your way of a happy life.

If I live my life as a journey to experience unconditional love, then it stands to reason that all events of my life are a part of that journey.

Pause. Pause. Pause.

This journey will possibly turn everything you thought up until now on its head. I'm not here to make you wrong or to judge your choices. Quite the contrary. I'm here to invite you into a new possibility: to reckon with your conflicting internal voices and distinguish between 1) the one that isn't telling you the truth, 2) the one that you think is you but is actually a set of judgments, and 3) your true voice.

Conflict is an opening. Pause. Consider what it would be like to entertain the thought that this moment – this conflict – is an opening. The ongoing series of fights, disagreements, pains, hurts, disconnections, and resulting distance between you...consider for a moment that these present you with an opening. A doorway you can choose to walk through now.

Contrast that path with another path, one that so many choose instead.

ANDREA

She walks down the self-righteous, judgmental, conflict-ridden, difficult, and hurtful path, making him wrong and making him pay for it. She would never say this out loud and would deny it if you confronted her. This path wasn't her intention. She did love him once. But, if the choice was between him or her, she was going to save herself. Especially as a mom, she needed to save herself so she could take care of her children. So, sorry, but screw him. So she found her community, her people who would tell her that it's OK, that he was a jerk, that he never deserved her, that he stopped her from living her best life... Even if he wasn't really a jerk, he didn't give her what she needed. While this kind of support didn't feel very good – her real needs were not met by the "love" her friends and family were giving her during this kind of consoling – it was better than nothing and helped her get up in the morning and keep going.

Conflict is an opening. This conflict. This moment in time. This opportunity. Conflict is an opportunity. What is it here to share with me? What is it here to tell me? What conflicts are the same as ones I've experienced in other relationships? Which conflicts have I been living over and over and over again? Not just in this marriage, but in previous marriages or previous relationships, or in my childhood and transition from childhood to adulthood? What conflicts have I been ignoring? Hoping, praying, and semi-successfully convincing myself that they were someone else's doing and the answer lied in getting away from them? Until the next conflict showed up.

How did you get here? Whether you are a fighter, flighter, or freezer, we all pretty much got here in the same way. So, you are among good company. No matter your strategy, the goal was to endure as little conflict as possible. Even for us fighters (yup, that's me), it's easy to judge us as wanting the conflict. We're told that we create conflict because we like it. In reality, it is a strategy no different from the flighters and freezers. We all want peace, relief, and avoidance of the pain. We're just using different strategies.

Pause. Conflict is an opening to understand, at a deeper level, the strategies we've been using up until now to avoid pain and discomfort. Why did we need strategies? Because we didn't know where the pain might take us. And the unknown is scary. Because we didn't know how to successfully navigate the discomfort. And we wanted to be successful. Because we thought he was the issue, and people and events convinced us that this was, in fact, reality. And it was easier to believe this than look in the mirror.

When I am in constant judgment of my experiences as either "good" or "bad," I am living a half-life.

The act of pausing is the first step in "The P-R-A-C-T-I-C-E." Pausing to notice our breathing, to recognize we are alive! To rejoice in that simple fact, so that we can begin to walk down another path. A path that enables us to see the events of our lives through different eyes. To begin the inquiry. To start to notice our judgments as separate from the event itself. To begin to show up in life as an observer. Conflict is an opening. It's a beautiful invitation to live our present, and even our past, in quite a different way than we have been. What's possible then?

Conflict is your invitation to start asking questions and hear your answers.

Refining and practicing the act of pausing is a tool that is essential in the process. In some ways, it's the beginning, the middle, and the end. It's a tool that will enable you to better hear yourself and others. I'll take a guess that one of the most painful experiences you've endured up until now is your husband's inability to hear you, the feeling that he's never really heard you. And, if I were to ask him, he would probably say the same thing about you.

Pausing allows us to get present so we can actually be with another. If you consider this, I wonder if it would begin to make sense that the distance between you and your husband, the man you once called the love of your life, is partly due to the fact that you did not feel listened to, heard, or understood. And if you weren't pausing to hear him, then you didn't hear him tell you the very same thing.

Pausing. Listening. Breathing. Receiving. The act of being in relationship with another is being present enough to receive him. Receive him as he is, not as you want him to be. Receive him as who he has become, receiving all that made him who he is, up until this very moment. Being in relationship is a series of moments: releasing, letting go, restarting, and questioning. My guess is that, while you may have been asking questions, your questions weren't really questions but rather disguised daggers, a veiled assault when you could not longer sit with your anger, disappointment, and frustration (or maybe that was just my strategy?).

Did you ever really know him? Did you ever really get so vulnerable with him that he could know you? Did you ever really know you? If not, did you believe he could know you, figure you out, if you didn't know yourself?

How do you begin to distinguish between what you judged about what happened and, what really happened?

Consider the following example. There are 12 children in a family sitting around the dinner table at Thanksgiving, listening to a story they are all fond of remembering; the day the youngest child was born. But, never had they all sat at this table as adults sharing this story together. Here's what happens. One sibling shares his version. Then another, then another. As they sit there laughing and enjoying the story, they are also arguing, gently, and insisting that other versions of the story are incorrect. He was born at 7 a.m. – no, 8 – no, 9 – etc. Dad was in the waiting room, no he was in the room with mom, no, he was at work on his way there, and so on. People's interpretations are different. Their memories are different. The younger ones remember situations in part based on their smaller sizes at the time. The older ones remember through the eyes of being surrogate parents with responsibility for the younger ones. Whose story is true? Even Mom and Dad in this scenario have different versions. That's fourteen versions of the same story!

When we sit down to consider what happened, initially, we simply want to acknowledge that there are many versions of the same story. Yours and his. There's the angry version, the victim version, the neutral version, the loving-wisdom version, and so on. One of the first things I do with clients is to listen for which version of the story they're telling. I hear husband's version, and wife's version, then the awkward version they tell in tandem the first time we sit together in the same room. Slowly, there is recognition that the version each of them tells is not the whole story, and some of it may not even be based on actual events.

What does this mean? Here's another example.

MATTHEW AND REBECCA

Matthew and Rebecca experienced the same conflict repeatedly, based on different versions of a story. It began when they met and shared a desire to live spontaneously, not by society's rules. Both in agreement with this way of living, they traveled as a couple, imagined they were living the dream, and paved their own paths. One day, however, Matthew discovered that he longed to put down roots and settle down while Rebecca continued to want to be free and go where the wind took her. They both agreed, at least at some point, that children and marriage weren't in the cards for them. Then, it happened – they got pregnant. It was unexpected, unplanned, and they didn't knowing how to have a conversation about this (reminding each other that they never really wanted kids when one was on its way just seemed cruel). So, what did they do? They got married, they settled down, and they had a child. Sometime later, not so long after these events occurred (accompanied by increasing conflict and misunderstandings), they each began to tell a version of a story. She got pregnant, he wasn't being careful, she made him get married, he made her settle down, and so on. Not too long after that, her unhappiness settled in, and it was his fault. His unhappiness settled in, and it was her fault. And in their effort to revive the love they once felt for each other, they had another child.

How did they get here? Is it making more sense now?

Different versions of the same story. The unhappiness they each felt was blamed on the actions and inactions of the other. Pause. Listen. Breathe. Receive. It is at this precise moment in a couple's "awakening to the events of their lives" that, if they can pause, they can begin to recognize where they went unconscious, or, at least, when they began to turn over the responsibility for their own happiness to another. The version of the story they each told underscored this as their reality. Otherwise, it would be too painful and too uncomfortable, requiring they each address the steps they had skipped – the hard questions not asked. To consider all possibilities: to have a child or not, to get married or not, to stay together or not, to acknowledge different intentions for couplehood and see if they could get on the same page, or not.

Pause, breathe, listen, receive. The pause is the first step in starting to take back responsibility for your life. Perhaps this will feel a bit strange at first. In American culture, we like the phrase, "Take back control of your life." But in my mind, that's such a different thing. Control comes from survival perspective (the very thing we are not committing to while reading this book). When we are in "survival mode" we are solely concerned with looking good, being in control, or being right. It's an act of fear, an act to disempower others and intended to maintain an illusion of control. It's an act of either/or, win/lose and good/bad positioning.

Taking back responsibility sounds like, "This is my life, it always has been, and even if I've experienced many things I would rather have not had, it's always been me showing up while others have come in and come out of my life – it's time for me to start considering this idea: "I'm the common denominator." As you do the practices and start to see patterns repeating in your relationships, being the "common denominator" might actually be a relief. Mentally, we know we can't control others, but emotionally, we've been living as if we can. Living as, "I am responsible for my experience," creates a shift. From this perspective, you can make different choices, see your life differently, seek your purpose, ask questions, engage, and so on. In doing so, you will come to understand how you got here so you can begin to ask, "Where am I going? How do I want to feel? And now what?"

EXERCISES

Writing

I love this practice because it costs nothing, you can do it anywhere and anytime, alone or with others, and it requires no new skills. Before writing this book, I spent almost 11 years (the time since my second divorce) writing. Writing eventually became a tool to communicate with clients and to serve. But, for many years, I used it as a tool to communicate with myself and to heal. There are four types of writing I've practiced over the years, which have produced life-changing results.

1. Soul writing. Try writing down a question with your dominant hand and responding with your other hand. Or, with your dominant hand, write a question to your "inner wisdom" or intuition, and allow your inner wisdom or intuition to respond. Do not pause to think about this process – otherwise, your brain will get in the way. The purpose of writing this way is to connect with your subconscious and begin to receive information beyond your conscious thinking process.

2. Freeform writing. Write without stopping – do not pick up your pen from the paper. You can scribble or write the same thing over, no editing, and no rereading. Then, burn or tear up the paper when you are done. The purpose of writing this way is to release energy and old stories. Keep writing until you feel complete.

3. Journaling. Having a journal or notebook nearby is useful to jot down thoughts as they come. Another way to work with a journal is to create a gratitude practice in the morning or evening, for five minutes a day, where you focus on the quality of your daily experiences. Having your journal near your bedside is a way to facilitate a practice when you first wake up

or before you go to sleep. In the morning, you might wish to write down what you remember from your dreams, as you may find that going through this process brings forward more dreaming.

4. Sentence prompts/creative writing. This practice is like freeform writing in that you do not pick up pen from paper, and you don't edit or read while you write. You can give yourself a prompt or find them on the Internet if you search for "writing prompts." The purpose of this type of writing is to start you on a path to access your creativity beyond your conscious thinking mind, and see where you end up. During a workshop focusing on grief and healing, here is where a prompt led me: "As I dove...."

As I dove into the water it felt cold and delicious, scary, curious and unknown. *And I went deeper and deeper until I could barely breathe and I thought I would never see the surface again. But I dove because I couldn't think of anything else to do. I dove because something inside me said go deeper, you're safe, seek, keep going. And so I dove. And I went deeper, and I found myself getting comfortable and acquainted with my new surroundings.*

I tested the waters so to speak and I moved one arm and then the other, felt the water absorb me, I felt covered, surrounded and I melted within it. I became the water, and I no longer knew where I started and it began. And it was ok. I wasn't scared, in the flow of the deep, I floated, I swam, I laughed and I cried. I tried to scream but all I could see were the ripples of the vibration from the waves that would have made sound had they touched air. I watched my hair float before my eyes, blocking my view at times, and for my hair and this pause from seeing out, I was grateful. I could stay here forever, floating, freely, no physical sensation. But an inner voice told me that I was only to be a visitor not a resident of this place. But it was available to me any time I wanted to visit. I felt grateful but sad and scared to return to the surface because that's where pain resided. I didn't want to return to that place, where all of my sensations would be alerted and I did not know how to float, or swim, or fly. I asked for guidance, it reassured me that I was safe above and below. That one place did not exist without the other, and my job was to learn to navigate fluidly, the journey between both places, when they called to me. This was reassuring to hear, and I understood. I thanked this deep, mys-

terious place and gently floated back to the sur-face. The cool air on my face at first shocking, then welcoming. This was home, my other home, among people, among the activity of life. I loved this place and faced it head on, grateful for the joy and the pain, the lessons and the healing. And that little voice spoke to me in this place, reminding me to return to the deep when it was time, and I would know when that time was. And I felt gratitude and peace. As above so below. Two halves of my life, one not better than the other, two parts compos-ing a whole. Embracing them both would allow me to fully integrate, be a whole woman.

Life As an Infinity Symbol

Draw an infinity symbol on a piece of paper a few times then pause (please do this before you con-tinue reading). Do you notice how the lines are mismatched as you do the motion over and over? Continue drawing for another minute or so (please do this before you continue reading). Did you no-tice that, at some point, a thick line forms? All the lines became aligned? Consider this practice as a metaphor for all the stuff you lived. At first, the events of our lives might seem mismatched, misaligned, and maybe useless. There are "good" lines and "bad" ones. Lines "in the box" and lines that have gone astray. Once enough lines are lived, however, a picture comes into place. When we see this, no matter our stories, our background, or our suffering, our individual infinity symbols eventually all look the same. How might you consider your life if you observed it through this lens?

Breathing

Our breath is our life energy. It's what brings us to life when we exit the womb and what exits our body as we stop functioning at death. How deeply and consciously we engage with our breath may be a metaphor for how deeply and consciously we're engaging with our lives. Our breathing connects us to life. Yet, many of us live much of our lives completely unconscious of what truly allows us to exist. Giving a little more attention to our breath, particularly in times of stress and conflict, supports us in pausing, being a little more present, and being in our bodies. Imagine you are in a terrible fight with someone you love. Rather than say the first thing that comes to mind and "put one more nail in the coffin," so to speak, you take ten deep breaths. Really sit with this one for a moment. Pause now and take ten deep breaths.

Notice anything differently? When I remember to do this practice, I feel my attention drawn to different places in my body, to emotional pain points, the anguish I feel in the midst of a fight, or the pain I feel in my body – the breath can actually address much of it. From this place, the discomfort we're experiencing softens ever so slightly. We are reminded on a physiological level that we're not running away from a tiger, and whatever we're facing will most probably not kill us. Mentally, emotionally, and physically, we're better suited to be with what is in front of us and return to a place where curiosity can exist. We are "rescued" from reactivity and potential destructive behavior, and invited into possibility.

There are many breathing techniques, and I am not an expert in this domain. Rather, I suggest that you begin by sitting with the question of how you can be more conscious with your breath (your own life) and get into a relationship with it. Look up apps on "pausing" and "calm" and "breathing," and go to YouTube and seek out videos on breathing techniques. Play with your breath by breathing deeply and exhaling forcefully, or taking shorter breaths and noticing your experience. Take a meditation or yoga class and notice the focus on breathing. Try closing your eyes and notice if you're paying more attention to your breath now. Count while breathing. See if your breath is even or staccato. Stand, sit, lie down, and notice the difference in your breathing. Place your hands on your chest, stomach, or belly – where does your air go, and what happens when you direct it elsewhere? Climb some stairs or do some sit-ups and notice how you breathe in action. Being in relationship with your breath is a tool you can use when conflict and discomfort arise. Remember, we cannot breathe big gulps and put them in a bank for later use. Our breath can be held only for so long until we must make a choice to take the next breath or die. Breath, therefore, is the ultimate indicator of how present we are and is perhaps our greatest gift in working with our discomfort and conflict.

Non-Judgment

We live in a judgmental world. It's in the air we breathe, and that air is killing us. Try practicing non-judgment for one day. Choose one day. When you wake up, speak the words to yourself, "I will judge nothing today. Rather, I will simply observe." As you walk through your day, repeat this like a mantra and simply notice. At the end of your day, consider journaling about your experience and, if you're up for it, plan to do this practice another day. In time, you become more aware of your tendency to judge in certain situations and with certain people. That awareness will assist you in moving more regularly into non-judgment. In this place, you increase your ability to be present, ask questions, listen, and receive.

Self-Forgiveness

It's not a natural thought. When we are in conflict, when we feel wronged, we claim, "He needs to apologize" or "I need an apology." This is looking to the outside for something we deeply need inside. Enter self-forgiveness. What if the very things we feel wronged for are reflections of the very things we believe, that we've judged about ourselves? Self-forgiveness is a tool by which we come to soften inside, to recognize that much of what we have experienced had little to do with what was being done to us, but rather, what we had been doing to ourselves (for many, many years in some instances).

We have been conditioned to believe that forgiveness is about someone else. He hurt me but I forgave him. She left me but I forgave her, and so on. Self-forgiveness has more to do with the blame, judgment, anger, and sometimes a violent attitude that we hold against ourselves when we think we have done something wrong. We call forth fire and rain upon us, chastising ourselves when we made a poor choice, brought ourselves into a bad situation, or blamed someone or something for our current circumstances. We think our anger is directed at the person or situation, and maybe it is at some point. But what happens after? Even if we avoid that situation or that person, the experience lingers within us until we process it. Self-forgiveness is saying you are ready to let go of what you are holding onto, that you don't need it anymore, and that you realize that the beliefs you had about the person or situation were a reflection of some belief you had about yourself.

How do you practice self-forgiveness? It begins quite simply, with a pause. Noticing what you're experiencing. When you find yourself judging externally (that will be your cue that you're judging something internally), pause, and consider making a statement such as, "I forgive myself for judging myself as..." or, "I forgive myself for judging him/her as...." Self-forgiveness has direct impact on our ability to walk through the world with an open heart and loving intentions. Consider using the practice of self-forgiveness any time you notice yourself judging yourself or others. Replace that judgment with loving intention so that it can be released.

Pause

We cannot judge and love at the same time.

In judgment, we cannot experience the vibration of love. This applies to loving yourself and loving another.

Conflict is an opening, and an opportunity for love and growth.

Constantly judging every experience as good or bad is not fully living within the spectrum of all of life's experiences. What would it look and feel like to remove judgment from the conflict you're currently experiencing?

CHAPTER 5

Getting Your Parents Out of the Bedroom

"Love is what we are born with.
Fear is what we have learned here."
– MARIANNE WILLIAMSON

"We do not learn from our experiences; we learn by reflecting on our experiences."
– JOHN DEWEY

The past can have a lock on us physically and emotionally. Which stories are true? False? Exaggerated? How do the stories handed down to you have bearing on you today? By reflecting upon all of the elements that make you you, there is a wealth of knowledge and information. Focusing on what we have learned from our own lives and the experiences and interpretations of the generations before us, our ability to receive and choose what we want to nurture in ourselves and in our families is strengthened.

STEP 2: REFLECT AND RECEIVE

Growing up, the evenings were quiet as we lived isolated from one another – my parents, my sister, and me. The weekends consisted of occasional family and friends visiting, and the inevitable melancholy, food, and complaining.

My father spent his formative years hiding from the Nazis, deprived of the nurturing and support of family and community. I never took that into consideration as the cause of his unhappiness because it was never talked about. He never said a word about it. When my parents were on the verge of separation, as they had been in some form or another for over a decade, my father sought counseling when my mother threatened to leave him if he did not. I'll always wonder what happened during those sessions. My mother reported that my father – as she heard from the therapist – would complain about her, play the victim, and take no responsibility. She heard that he was doing it for her because he couldn't do it for himself. He was scared and confused, and his pain ran so deep no one could ever touch it. My mother, on the other hand, wanted help, and yet her strategy was not unlike his – blaming her unhappiness on him. After all those sessions, she gained the courage to leave him, but not quite the wisdom to know why. While she took steps towards creating her own future, twenty-eight years without my father did not prove to be the answer to her unhappiness.

Growing up I learned the art of subtle victimhood.

It was all around me. The aunt who came every weekend and complained that life had given her an unfair deal – and if you contradicted her, watch out. Her husband suffering mostly in silence, but you knew the reason for his unhappiness. My parents were in some way the same and opposites. They fit roles for each other – the cause of the unhappiness of the other – while they avoided the harder questions. What makes me happy? Was I ever happy? Who am I when it's just me? What are my thoughts? Who am I beyond the sum of my parents? Am I running towards them or away?

My father's father was an abusive alcoholic and my father's mother was considered a saint. Yet, my grandmother suffered and never had much regard for herself. Her family loved her and looked up to her, but I wonder if she found that odd, as her life was mostly about sacrificing for others. Is that a life to look up to? To aspire to? Do we have to suffer and give everything to reach sainthood? Is this life not for each of us?

I don't think my parents had the Cinderella story in their heads. They were simply two people looking to escape. Amongst the nuns, my mother's indoctrination included strict Catholic practices: austerity, charity, and coldness. She found refuge in what limited creations she dared to explore: art, music or laughter. My father, his abusive father, and his impoverished state as a Jew in a country that did not welcome him was, at seven years old, running for his life, hiding for his life, foraging for his life. Escaping the Nazis would lead him into an adulthood conditioned to distrust even circumstances that were beautiful: two beautiful healthy children, a successful career as a doctor, and the admiration of his community. Happiness eluded him and so too, my mother, as the doctor's wife and hopeless romantic.

This was a good life, potentially, but the circumstances from which they came to this life kept them captive. Until they understood those circumstances, they would forever be captive.

We have been attempting to break out of a system that was never based on love and healing.

My father died at age 59 when I was 22, and my mother at age 67 when I was 45. Cancer took both of them. Pause.

Cancer ate parts of their bodies, his heart, her breast, his spine, her hip, his lungs, her skin. Their unresolved emotional states and unhappiness ate away at them as well. Of course, they did not see it that way, because I believe if they had, they might have made other choices. But I learned from them. I believe we can all learn from them.

A life of subtle victimhood cannot help but eat at your vitality, life energy, health, generosity, and mind. Little by little, it's so subtle that one day you don't recognize yourself and you ask, "How did I get here, and where is *here*?"

A million little choices – some yours, some your parents, a hundred misunderstandings, misbeliefs, hundreds or thousands of messages you've heard along the way – falsely convincing you of who you are. You believed because you were a baby, then a toddler, then an adolescent. When it was time to leave your family, to individuate from your parents, you were so conditioned, and still so much a part of them. Of them. How could you truly know what was you, and what was them – what you wanted to keep and live by, and what you wanted to discard? How could you know?

You left home and lived on your own – maybe went to college or got married, maybe had children. Through these life experiences, you tried to live something similar or different. You told yourself, "I'll never do that like my parents," or, "I want to do it exactly like them." But either way, you were living in response to them. There were a million little choices that you thought were choices, but were they really?

A subtle victim is reacting without knowing the true cause.

When I was three, I understood that my parents were unhappy. Only unhappy parents, only parents who themselves had not healed their demons and the monsters that lived under their beds, could stand by when part of their child disappeared inside herself. The cause was a silly incident that would inform the trajectory of my life. There we were, my sister and I, in the hallway of our new house, with crayons and a wall. Who knows what inspired us to draw on those walls (with glee I might add). You can guess what happened next. My mother stood by as my father lost it. Was it the perceived disrespect of a child? Was it that he worked so hard coming from nothing to see his walls now defaced? Was it like the defacement of the buildings in Paris when the Nazis came through? I'll never know. But I can remember like it was yesterday (in my heart, bones, and flesh), the terror I felt at my father's hand. I could not speak – it felt like sand filling up my throat – and I could not breathe. I would relive this feeling in other experiences in my life: falling down the stairs as a child only hours after my parents left on vacation, leaving me breathless; during an altercation with a boyfriend, a partner, a husband, leaving me breathless again and again and again.

We all have our stories, and to understand how we got here is to understand where it began.

The crayon story was a pivotal moment I remember more in my body than in my mind. It was a moment when the king and queen, my benevolent parents, became the evil emperor and his empress who stood by while he carried out his reign. I no longer felt safe. I was afraid to make mistakes, so I became an "A" student. I screamed and yelled for attention, but my heart was never revealed or attended to. I began using many strategies from that day forward to live in that house and survive. The moment I felt unsafe I could not truly thrive.

Yet, I longed. I longed for the version of our family that other families told. I was the doctor's daughter. We had the house on the hill. We were the "two parents, two kids" nuclear family – the intact family, a family that was admired from afar. We "should" have been happy by all accounts. We had our food, shelter, and clothing. We did not need to worry about our basic survival, which, in some ways, made it that much more complicated. What did *we* really have to complain about?

The practice of reflection is our ability to look back on the events of our lives with compassion, inquiry, and a desire for understanding. It's a practice of digging underneath our perceived notions (judgments) and asking what this information has in store for us. It invites us to ask how we can learn and understand how we got here, as opposed to judging the past and being angry for where we are and what we've experienced. Reflection follows the pause. It requires a willingness to be with what was and what is, to learn about the people and places, to wonder what happened to them. It asks that we explore "ancestral lines" of beliefs and stories and the accompanying emotions. Reflection invites us into a deeper listening of ourselves, to begin a relationship with our intuition or develop one. Reflection. There is an interdependent relationship between your past and your present, and between your parent's histories and your history with your husband; just as there was a history between your parents and their parents that informs you today, though you may not yet have enough information to understand how. While we heard many stories growing up – or, as in my case, felt them – they are not as significant as the beliefs, judgments, and misunderstandings that exist because of them.

Reflection is an opening then, to receive all of the information that has always been there. Engaging in this second practice of reflection and receiving is literally telling our subconscious and unconscious that we are ready to listen.

EXERCISES

Listening

Many people don't listen very well. With all we have going on in our lives, we struggle to even be present. Imagine how much more effort or surrender it takes to be still, stand before a person, shut off the mind, and listen. I believe this is an act of receiving the other person. As you come to understand how you got here, listening will be a practice you engage in regularly and consciously. The act of listening refers to numerous ways in which you'll do this practice. First and foremost, it's listening to yourself. The practice of reflection is actually an act of listening to yourself, the stories, the past, your childhood, your family history, and your intuition. It's listening for that little voice that's always been there but wasn't loud enough for you to hear, or maybe you ignored it, or denied it. It's an act of listening internally when you ask questions and trust that the answers lie within. Listening while reflecting is a way to tap into source or spirit (or from wherever you derive your wisdom and intuition). These are perhaps the most significant ways of listening, and as we move into more personal responsibility for our lives, this internal listening will be vitally important.

Three distinctions to consider:

1. What am I listening to?
2. What am I listening for?
3. How am I listening?

There is the externally-focused listening to the people around you – perhaps most importantly to your husband, children, parents, colleagues, and friends – but also to the world around you: the land, the trees, and the environment. It's listening to receive the information that is swarming around you. A simple way of doing this with another is to set a timer for five minutes, sit in front of each other (knees touching) and making eye contact. One person shares for five minutes while the other practices listening. While you are the listener, soften your mind and notice if you have an urge to respond. Let the thoughts come and go as you continue to listen and receive the person sitting in front of you as they share. Once the five minutes are up, it's the other person's turn to share. Repeat the exercise. While five minutes may feel like a short time, clients report that doing this practice daily creates connection and intimacy. Five minutes of sharing and listening with intention can actually feel like a long time.

Personal Responsibility

Personal responsibility has been given a bad rap, because too often it is associated with guilt, burden, and obligation. I resisted those words as much as the next person. But the moment I heard a teacher say, "Responsibility is the ability to respond," my world changed. My idea up until then was that responsibility was a heavy, difficult, and guilt-inducing word. The ability to respond, however, created freedom, an opening. It reminded me that, in any given moment, I am not victim of the people and situations around me or of my past. Rather, I am a conscious human being who has access to choices. No matter what happened or was happening, I have the ability to choose how I act and how I respond. This enabled me to unshackle from ways of being that I thought were simply conditioned into me. "The angry girl," "the obstinate girl," and "the undisciplined girl" were labels that had been placed on me, convincing me that I was basically doomed. So, of course, it would follow that I needed to shield myself from the weight of responsibility for being such a bad person and find ways to blame my world. This created many relationships where I did not have the capacity to respond from a place of choice, reinforcing my "subtle victimhood." The minute I spoke the words, "He wasn't nice to me," "He wasn't being responsible," or, "He hurt me," I was putting my experience on *him*. I wheedled myself out of needing to be proactive. Subsequently, I was able to create the changes I was capable of making to experience something different, rather than leaving it up to the other person. And who wants to take on my responsibility? No one does. The result?

The relationships would either live in patterns of continued, unresolved conflict, or they would end.

Personal responsibility is our freedom! While practicing the idea, "I am responsible for everything," we practice expanding how we walk through the world. We see solutions when others only see problems. We begin to become the authors of our lives and our experience. We create room to fully have our experience and invite others to have theirs! We begin to create spaciousness between you and me, with room to co-exist. It's not an either/or and it's not a compromise. It's a fundamental shift in how each of us walks through the world. It's autonomy in the healthiest of senses. It's freedom. It's space.

A New Relationship with Time

In traditional western schools, we are taught timelines that are often linear. In the practice of reflection and receiving, time shifts. Events that occurred years or decades ago can become significant in the present day as you explore and inquire about them. Creating a new relationship with time means acknowledging that your childhood experiences have present-day impact. It's this resonance with the past that will ultimately help you heal, repair and grow. We are a whole of our parts: our little girl, our teenage self, the success and the failures, and the wins and losses. As we reflect and receive, those memories and experiences become information to help understand the patterns and grooves that have been deeply created, and inform the decisions we are currently making. So, when a client says to me, "I'm leaving him because he takes no personal responsibility for anything," my first instinct is to inquire about when the pattern began and keep digging from there. When was it too scary or too much for him to own his role in a situation? When a couple is willing to engage in this inquiry, there is gold to be found, transforming their conflict into an opportunity for understanding and compassion. I trust 100 percent that one or many events and deeply grooved patterns from each of their pasts are informing their actions today.

The events I share throughout this book span five decades. What I understood as a child, teenager, or young adult is vastly different than what I understood in my 20s, 30s, and 40s. The gift of time shows us that, when we are ready to understand, we do. You'll know because you'll feel it in your bones. Creating a new relationship with time ultimately means having patience. Allow for the time. Recognize the value of time.

Seven-Year Conflict Exercise

In this exercise, you will reflect on and receive all of this beautiful, messy material that is available to you by reviewing your life in seven-year cycles and reflecting on what was happening just before the seventh year and just after: the changes, conflicts, and transitions. In considering your seven-year cycles, you will come to see that there are patterns which emerge.

Recalling your stages starting with the age of 7, and then 14, 21, 28, and so on can be quite informative. If you don't recognize any patterns, then the practice of writing down what was happening during these stages and reflecting on them will be informative. It will assist you in understanding how you got here and what made you, you, so that you can take the next steps in choosing the parts you will develop, the parts you will heal, and the parts you will release.

When you find pain or fear associated with an experience, it's perfectly understandable to want to shy away from it, maybe even bury it. But it then becomes buried and negative experiences that will come back time and time again with other people in other situations. I've observed this in my own life and with clients in their first, second, and third marriages, and through multiple relationships and break-ups – different people, similar results. We must admit that pushing away the past is hurting us, disabling our ability to be with the person in front of us, and limiting our ability to thrive in relationship. History repeats itself. We plead, "How can this be happening again?" The answers lie in doing these exercises.

On time and multitasking, Scott M. Peck said, "You cannot truly do anything else and listen to someone at the same time." Perhaps in recent history, this is more relevant than ever. Balancing relationships, parenting, marriage, working, bills, a house, friends, family, and so many commitments alongside the ever-increasing amount of information that we must prioritize and decipher, puts listening in the back seat. We find it perfectly normal to check our phones during conversation and talk with our loved ones while we engage in another task, and to insist that we don't have time for one reason or another.

We have enough time. There is always enough time. The question to ask is, "What does my use of time say about how and what I choose to prioritize?" Consider that a new relationship with time informs you of what is worth taking a stand for and what is important enough to pause, listen, and receive.

Reflection and Receiving

The practice of Reflection and Receiving is our ability to look back on the events of our lives with compassion, inquiry, and a desire for understanding. This includes questioning judgments and having clarity about how we arrived where we are now, rather than remaining stuck, angry, and living in the past.

Reflection follows the pause. We need that pause so we don't skim through the valuable information and avoid the pain and fear of emotions that well up in us. When we go deep with our feelings, we can lay them to rest, forgive the past and experience relief.

Reflection invites us into a deeper listening of ourselves, our childhoods, our family history, and our intuition. There is an interdependent relationship between your past and your present, among your parent's histories and their parents, as well as the ancestral lines of your mate. This history informs how you live today.

Personal responsibility is a present-day, conscious and empowered ability to choose how you will act, respond, and live your life the way you wish to experience it. This releases blame we put on others for disappointments when life didn't turn out like we thought it should, and enables us to own our part in it. Personal responsibility is our freedom!

CHAPTER 6

The Dance of Laughter and Sorrow

"We can only learn to love by loving."
– IRIS MURDOCH

"To a mind that is still, the whole world surrenders."
– LAO TZU

Starting at a young age, resistance can close us down. Later on in life, and paired with your spouse, the resistance builds, blocking listening and meaningful connection. We can be quite creative with our excuses stemming from our childhood resistance—shoring up old patterns to avoid loss of freedom and control while we hang on to being "right." In resistance, we prolong these fights with ourselves, our spouse, and the world. By disassembling the walls we believed were protecting us, we begin to navigate conflict with the realization that it is here to teach us something.

STEP 3: ACCEPT AND ACKNOWLEDGE

When did all of my resistance start? Where does the conflict come from? Why can't I find my happiness?

What were the origins of your conflict story? When was the first time you can remember being in conflict? Was it with a parent? A schoolyard fight? Watching something on the TV that made you judge someone or, worse, judge yourself?

Conflict is an internal and external experience. How we approach that experience is at the heart of determining the correct choices for your life. As you become more observant of your experience, the patterns and strategies you used in your life to navigate conflict, discomfort, and transition become more apparent. Eventually, this will lead you to a "reframing" of your experience of conflict.

Your conflict story is the unique set of ideas, misbeliefs, interpretations, strategies, and stories you've told yourself to survive your circumstances. The good news is we all have one. The bad news is that delving into your individual story will bring up the very thing your story has been trying to protect you from – conflict, discomfort, potential change, and transition.

Where to begin? If you have done some of the practices in Chapters 4 and 5, you have already begun to see certain patterns and beliefs you held and lived up until now. At this stage, it's time to take a broader look at your conflict attitude or approach. Are you a fighter? A flighter? A freezer? Do you avoid conflict at all costs, or do you jump in, hoping to quell your inner discomfort by dealing with it in the moment, often to the dismay of a flighter or freezer who had no desire to deal with it in the moment? On that, we'll often see we attract people with different strategies, which adds another layer to the conflict.

VALERIE AND ROBERT

Robert and Valerie spent most of their time in conflict around money. Valerie was a saver, and Robert was a spender. Valerie was always thinking 20 years out, while Robert wanted to be spontaneous and live in the moment. When they came to me, they wanted help navigating their money conflicts – which showed up in every area of their family life. When we dug a little deeper, Valerie shared that she was most often the instigator of these conversations, while Robert did everything to avoid them. What they came to understand was that their fights were not really about money, but rather, how Robert avoided discussions about money for fear they would turn into fights. Valerie, a self-proclaimed "fighter," feared the consequences of never having the discussion, and thus pushed the conversation/conflict every chance she got. Digging even deeper, both Robert and Valerie revealed the underlying issues they were most desperate to avoid – unresolved childhood hurts and misunderstandings that had informed decades of patterns in their relationship. Their "money conflicts" served as distractions and enabled them to avoid the deeper pains.

The conflict, in this case, revolved around the survival strategy as opposed to addressing the underlying issue at hand.

Once you begin to understand how you've been approaching conflict, then you can work at that level, individually, and come to have an easier and more graceful relationship with the idea and practice of being in conflict. You can now distinguish between the context and the content of the conversation. In Robert and Valerie's case, they would eventually work to make conscious and intentional money decisions based on their shared values (addressing the "content" they were working with – money). But the "context" was the key to being able to get there. Context is our semi-conscious or unconscious thoughts, feelings, underlying stories, and beliefs that trigger our fight, flight, or freeze response. It's the backdrop to any conflict we're experiencing. Always in the background our context informs how we'll approach the conflict.

THEO AND AMY

Theo and Amy were married for seven years when they came to see me. On the brink of divorce and barely able to have a conversation without tears or angry words, they believed the only option was to separate, to stop the pain and regain some hope for their happy futures individually. Theo complained that Amy wasn't very present, was always angry and critical with him, and that he felt like he could never be good enough for her. Amy complained that all she wanted was for Theo to be happy, but for years he complained about his job and took no steps to change it. Instead, he engaged in unhealthy diversion tactics like drinking and gambling to avoid the harder choices. On the surface, it looked like they weren't on the same page and that their values and dreams for the future were different. After working together for a few weeks (their relationship getting worse before it got better), Theo and Amy discovered that their pattern of engagement was motivated by deeper fears and unresolved childhood patterns. Amy's strategy was to fight, Theo's was to flee. When we dived underneath the surface, Amy came to understand that unresolved issues with her stepfather and mother (who were alcoholics) played a part in her severe criticism of Theo's drinking. Theo's childhood informed their marriage dynamic as he had grown up in a household where difficult conversations were avoided, and little intimacy was shared with his parents and siblings. Theo and Amy's strategies – flight and fight – were what they were fighting about instead of focusing on a bigger picture and doing some healing and repair work. Addressing the past together, they were able to mourn several miscarriages and see each other as a true partner in healing and unconditional loving. As they delved beneath their patterns and areas of resistance, they found empathy and compassion and were able to recommit to a life together.

Once you know your conflict story (reference the seven-year conflict cycle exercise in the previous chapter), and your unique (or not-so-unique approach) to conflict, then what? It's time to reframe conflict itself.

This means being open to the possibility that conflict itself is something to embrace. It means that you welcome the discomfort, because it's telling you that something doesn't feel aligned. Once you become conscious of your core values and what matters to you most, that discomfort will be useful and valuable information, because it helps you keep on track. Discomfort tells you that something needs to change. Discomfort tells you that there is a greater possibility.

Discomfort is an invitation to the next level of intimacy, growth, spiritual development, and unconditional loving.

Conflict and discomfort then become something more than the emotions or physical and mental experiences we associate with them. Conflict is a state of mind. The question is what state of mind might support you best in navigating your life that is naturally bound up with healthy doses of discomfort, conflict, change, and transition? Do you get angry when the seasons change? Are you upset when you see a caterpillar struggling to free itself from its cocoon to become a butterfly? Or, do you recognize that the caterpillar is simply in its experience, intuitively acknowledging that the struggle is part of its natural process? Seen through this lens, conflict and discomfort are natural. The more you can embody this principle, the more capacity you will have to expand your life by being with what is and then being able to say, "Now what?" – not from a place of reaction or limited possibilities because you're in judgment or resistance, but rather from a neutral place where any possibility exists, and you get to choose. Whatever your choice, you no longer think from a place of right or wrong. Instead, you consider, inquire, and choose.

As you acknowledge the origins of your conflict story, you will find yourself going deeper into the moment where some of the energy, tension, and remaining judgments can slowly fade away. There may be more that will come up in following months and years. Your practice and embodiment of this now will serve you well to go deeper into healing your story and taking ownership of your experience.

Your healing leads you to acceptance: understanding where your parents, their parents, your husband, your husband's parents, and their parents come from. By seeing with non-judgmental eyes all of this life experience, you can now understand how you got here, where you are, and how you can open yourself up to a greater possibility, because you are no longer resisting the past or the present.

You can be with what is and accept what is.

Can you imagine a life where you not only embrace all the conflict and discomfort you've experienced up until now, but also welcome it? Can you imagine a life where you are so present that you might not even know a great difference between your comfort and discomfort? A life where you are so present that you're not judging your experience but simply living it? This is what's possible now.

Included in the step of accepting and acknowledging is the idea of spaciousness and softening. Ideas, judgments, attachments, and beliefs can make us hard. They are solid. They are things we attach to. We may gravitate towards them because we live in a physical world and we want hard evidence. We want solid ground. We want clarity. Uneven ground brings up unsteadiness, like being in an earthquake.

Spaciousness and softening, however, do not only have to be an idea or a belief. They can be a state of being. As we move into acknowledging and accepting, our hearts and minds are more available to be with what is. Thus creating spaciousness, softening, and a shift in our listening.

In this state, you hear things you could not hear before. Your listening will be about receiving rather than reinforcing beliefs and ideas you insist are true. By softening and creating spaciousness in relationships, you start to see the possibility of what it means to come to "relationship present." Your expectations diminish and so does your neediness. Your need to be right, be in control, or "look good" diminishes because you are no longer in scarcity mode. You're not fleeing, fighting, or freezing. Suddenly, you will see that your life, your past and even your spouse will start to look differently. You'll ask, "When did that happen? When did that change?" The answers will surprise you, as nothing changed but your perspective. Spaciousness and softening now live within you, and you will want to continue cultivating them as you move forward.

EXERCISES

Explore a New Way of Doing an Old Thing

If you've ever moved, this experience will feel familiar to you. You're in a new city you might have visited once or twice before, maybe even more than that. But moving there is a new experience, and in order to live in this new place, you'll need to get acquainted and situated. Upon arrival, you show up at your new house or apartment, and everything is new. The house/apartment itself, the neighbors, perhaps the architecture, and the weather. You get in your car and start to drive around. You're literally reorienting yourself in this new place, and everything is new. There's so much you don't know: how to get from A to B, to your new home, to perhaps your new job or school, to your children's school, or to the grocery store. At the beginning, you'll use a phone app to check on directions and make sure you're headed in the right direction. After a few days or weeks or months, you'll find you no longer need the directions because these new routes and this new place is now familiar. You'll think to yourself, "I'm here, it feels good, and I know my way around. It's starting to feel like home." You'll feel like that for some time, enjoying getting acquainted with this new place, until one day it bothers you for some reason – the neighbors or the commute – and you might long for the place from which you came, or to go to a new place, or you may just complain about where you are. If you don't have some different thoughts or a novel experience, complaining, longing for the past, or longing for some other exciting new future might become your new normal.

This scenario resembles what we do in relationships. If we don't do something differently, we get stuck. The practice of doing something differently is to retrain your brain to see an old thing in a new way. In the above metaphor, you could take a different route to your kid's school or the supermarket, or drive around one day and get lost, or go to a place you've never been but were always curious about. This can actually transform the way you're experiencing the place in which you live and get you excited about it, or perhaps simply show you something new. It may inspire gratitude because you find a beautiful surprise at the end of that exploration, or it may confirm for you that it's time to move on and follow your intuition that says you are finished with this experience and something else awaits. Doing something differently works the same in relationship! Explore a new way of being in your relationship, with yourself or your husband, by doing this practice. It will involve pausing, inquiring, and receiving. Begin a ritual – maybe try date night again or read something to each other before bed. Ask for something you've never asked for. The possibilities are endless.

Open-Ended Questions

As we get more comfortable with the idea of noticing and observing, judgment will begin to feel strange. We'll notice when we're judging, and it won't feel correct anymore. Inquiry furthers our emotional and spiritual development in this realm. The practice of inquiry invites us to be in and live the questions, to acknowledge:

- what we know we know
- what we know we don't know
- what we don't know we know, and
- what we don't know we don't know

Inquiry says, "Any fixed idea I might have had yesterday, and bring into today, determines how I think today." Perhaps it seems silly, the idea of changing from day to day, but believe me, I've seen this in my work. People do change, and it can be from one day to the next. So, the practice of inquiry is simply to ask more questions. Open-ended questions are the best. For example: "Tell me more about that," "Help me to understand that," "What were you thinking there?" "Where were you going with that?" You'll notice, after practicing this skill more regularly, that questions requiring yes or no answers will begin to feel strangely limiting and do not invite greater inquiry. As we seek deeper intimacy, inquiry underscored by true interest, is a direct path to serving that end.

Gratitude

How we see a situation is how we'll experience the situation. Remember the crayon story? I didn't enjoy or appreciate that experience when I was having it, but can you see the growth and understanding that came from further reflection? Doing the practices makes this possible for all of us. Ultimately, the goal is to lean into gratitude for the experience; to embrace and understand the story yields great information and wisdom. Since it's your story, your job is to ask questions until the message becomes clear. In so doing, gratitude even for the ability to be in the question of what the meaning might be, is a great practice, and helps to soften and remove the judgments.

Gratitude plays an important role in helping to see that the world is not right/wrong or good/bad. One practice here is to find three things to be grateful for in a person with whom you're having conflict. In the process of finding these qualities, soften into some of the other practices (compassion and non-judgment) and, once again, you're presented with an opportunity to see this person or situation in another light. Easier said than done? Yes!!!! Because I'm a lifelong learner, I get to practice this on a regular basis. Not so long ago, I experienced a particularly uncomfortable conflict and used this practice.

It started when a potential new client called me. Urgency, fear, and worry marked our conversation as he was anxious to get a parenting plan together prior to his ex leaving the state. As they were never legally married, they weren't required to move through the court system via divorce, so their agreements until that moment were made verbally and loosely managed.

Less than 24 hours later, they were in my office, sitting down to have a challenging conversation. Due to the expediency of the process, I skipped steps, such as speaking with both people prior to this joint session, laying out the terms of how I work and what I charge, and managing expectations for a rushed process. By the end of the session, which was sprinkled with tense moments as they were not on the same page about what would be covered, they arrived at a series of agreements and had made some progress in their communication.

Fast-forward a few days and a few missed client calls, I receive a lengthy and scathing email from the mom, questioning my fees, process, and professional integrity. I never received such a well-written and well-thought out email from a client that was equal parts hurtful and doubting.

I used my breath.

I dug deep.

I reread it a few times.

Without reacting, I used inquiry. Rereading the email, I found that she very much valued our time together. In fact, she shared that it was the first time in years that they were able to see each other with some compassion and really listen to each other.

I called the dad and heard from him that this was mostly the point of view of his ex. He was very satisfied with the session. Perception checking to get a sense of where we all were, his was a piece of information that informed how I would then approach the next step, calling the aggrieved ex-partner. Ugh... breathe.

I remembered my own words of wisdom.

Feedback is information, and information is a gift. Therefore, this person is giving me a gift.

After a 30-minute phone call, there was a gift. By receiving feedback, working with my emotional and physical body to rise above the fight response (remember, that's my go-to), I could really listen.

The words I heard were powerful. There was acknowledgement, appreciation, and even a desire to possibly work with me in the future. There was a need for recognition for all those missed steps I mentioned above and how they impacted the process. It was an important reminder for me about why I have business practices in place and how I risk unpredictable results when I don't follow them. I recognized how I might serve clients more effectively if I were to take some of their thoughts into consideration.

In the end, through pausing, breathing, getting curious and listening, there was connection, kindness, appreciation, resolution, and repair. We left the conversation experiencing gratitude for each other and for the role that conflict played in these interactions. The power of gratitude.

Self-Love

Ahhh, self-love. Easier said than done, right? What does it even mean? Is it practicing self-care? Self-honoring choices? Is it getting curious about one's desires or the act of acknowledging one's desires? Yes, yes, yes, yes, and yes. Self-love begins when we can start embracing the entirety of our story. Self-love is a practice you can engage in wherever you are. It was an act of self-love to pick up this book, consider the words within, and do some of the practices.

Self-love is a way of declaring "me first:" my thoughts, my choices, my path, and my purpose. Self-love can be practiced in many ways. You may have physical practices, such as walking, swimming, yoga, seeing friends, napping, reading, and hiking (well, I guess those are mine when I practice them!). There are mental practices, such as reading and learning something new in a class or having interesting conversations that challenge your thinking and expand your point of view. It can be practices that work with your emotional landscape, for instance, listening to music that makes you feel a range of emotions or spending time with children or babies and connecting with their purity as their joy uplifts yours. It can be a good cry or a good laugh, or maybe it's exploring your feelings with a coach or therapist. Spiritually, self-love is a journey of coming to know that you are significant, and you belong; that there is perfection in your experience. It means that you were meant to be here and that there is a reason for your experience. It's acknowledging that your journey is, in fact, that – a journey. Your spiritual self-love may also lead you down a path of conscious co-creation with source, spirit, God, energy, or the universe. How ever you choose to practice self-love, remember that it is a practice that invites you to begin dreaming again.

Accept and Acknowledge

Once we address our resistance, we can examine the avoidance patterns and strategies we've built up throughout our lives to deal with conflict: the misbeliefs and the stories we make up about ourselves and others that soothe us but keep us stuck.

Knowing your conflict story from childhood can help you reframe what conflict actually means for you and for your partner. To develop an ability to "be with" disagreements and change is about listening, releasing the need to be right, and getting to an internal place of neutrality that can eventually soften into gratitude and appreciation for the conflicts themselves.

CHAPTER 7

The Death of Curiosity

"The only true voyage of discovery...would be not to visit strange lands but to possess other eyes."
- MARCEL PROUST

C uriosity and Courage have been severely underrated concepts. To be authentic requires courage. To be calm and centered means letting go of our "embarrassing mistakes." Being a witness to this authenticity means becoming *curious* about other people instead of jumping to conclusions. Be gentle with your judgments. Be inquisitive and grateful for the wonders of our emotional range and the freedom to express all of what and who we are.

STEP 4: CURIOSITY AND COURAGE

Some years ago, while perusing the sushi section at Whole Foods, and quite preoccupied on the multitude of choices, I noticed a little boy to my left. He was perhaps two years old kneeling in child's pose forehead to the ground, when he suddenly began to wail. It was a deep, sorrowful sobbing, not the whiny wailing of not getting a toy. He wailed and I watched. The whole scene pulled on my heartstrings. He wailed and I was amazed. I noticed a man who I assumed was his grandfather standing by, still and quiet. I was so moved by this scene. Lots of people would have picked up the child, maybe given him a slap on the butt or a hug, or forced him into acceptable supermarket behavior (I had been there, and done that...). Standing there, I watched with all the courage, kindness, and compassion it took for the grandfather to allow this child to experience this – whatever "this" was.

After what felt like a long time, but was probably only a few minutes, the little boy's mother joined the grandfather. She stood there quietly too. I looked at other people. Some looked disgusted while others seemed compassionate and understanding. "Been there..." I could imagine them musing. As more time went by I couldn't look at the sushi and couldn't think about lunch.

All I could do was stand still, in the presence of a fully lived experience. I was in awe. No words were exchanged, no punishment doled out. These two extraordinary adults just allowed this child his experience.

Thinking back to my childhood, I can feel the impact of hundreds, if not thousands, of stunted experiences. "Don't talk so loudly, don't cry, stop that." When, on rare occasion I fell ill, my parents would quickly assess and disregard. Somehow they knew how I felt and they always insisted I felt better than I really did. We have all experienced the minimizing of our pain – a fall, a tumble off the bike, the kind but uncomfortable urging of a parent telling us to get up, that it's not so bad – or more extreme – "Stop crying, you're not a baby."

While any caring parent might think it a kind act to shift a child's attention away from pain to something more pleasurable, or at least neutral, I'm equally confounded by the denial of another type of experience: joy. In a restaurant with my family, sharing a rare pleasant moment togeth-er, something funny happened or was said – I can't remember. I laughed and laughed, uproar-ious laughter coming from my solar plexus – a laugh that was commented on throughout my life: hardy (hearty!), deep and joy-filled. This time, however, it was criticized. "Be quiet," my father, under his breath, admonished me with a kind of ferocity that conveyed he meant business. The joy dissipated. I was silenced. I wanted to cry, but he would have been even angrier if I did. So, I held my breath (breathless yet again) and wished for the feelings to pass as quickly as possible to avoid the pain underneath. I shoved some food into my mouth.

As children, we wanted our parents to change. As parents, we want our children to behave differently. As husbands and wives, sisters and brothers, employers and employees, why are we so afraid, resistant, stubborn, and unwilling to allow ourselves and others to fully experience our experience?

The little boy showed me the beautiful symmetry and resolution in simply allowing the experience of the emotion. But, in order to do so, we must confront our discomfort and act with courage.

Are you willing to courageously witness your husband's pain and discomfort without acting to change or control it to console your own discomfort?

Here's what will be required:

- Courage to choose to be curious
- Courage to choose how you see this situation
- Courage to risk seeing it another way
- Courage to live your experience and let others lives theirs
- Courage to be present in the face of the discomfort
- Courage to show up and ask the hard questions
- Courage to be 100% responsible and see what that feels like
- Courage to dive into your heart to find what your truth is
- Courage to make a choice and live with the consequences
- Courage to act from a place of neutrality

It takes courage to stand in the face of discomfort, to be in the presence of someone else's discomfort and not move to soothe your own discomfort by quelling or fixing or reacting. Instead, it means having the courage to see with new eyes. You are now beginning to embody the idea that it's all serving a purpose, so the need to diminish, reduce or extinguish uncomfortable situations or feelings can begin to dissipate.

To be courageous, we must first create internal permission. It's having an inner awareness, a way of walking in the world that says, "I will find ways to remove distractions – people, substances, etc. – and create room to experience my experience. *I create this.* I claim this. I allow others the dignity of their experience."

Second, there's a "re-training" in how you relate to your spouse (and everyone else) that needs to happen. "Please sit and listen in loving witness. Don't comment, shrug, push me away, or react. I will do the same for you. We'll learn how to do this together and thereby help each other experience, fully, our individual experiences." We need to train ourselves to do this and then lead by example. You create the fertile ground that is the spaciousness to be with what is. It's a practice that may at first feel foreign and strange. You may need to warn people around you that you're not going to avoid the discomfort when something comes up. It's self-love that you stay with it, even if it looks like it's making others uncomfortable, and you, in turn, uncomfortable. In this way, you "recondition" yourself to more fully live your experiences. In so doing, you create permission for others to do the same.

Third, reintegrate courage and curiosity in your daily life. Learn how to be with the pain and feel it completely so that the experience can be complete. We've been living half-lives because we haven't allowed ourselves, for various reasons, to fully experience our experiences. To be present to the experience either wasn't allowed or wasn't exemplified to us by those we were learning from. Or, it was too scary, so we turned away from the experience. Our bodies and minds are filled with half-lived experiences, because those experiences are still lingering somewhere inside.

Resentment, for example, is a half-lived experience – old anger, similar to thoughts such as "He should have, or she didn't." It's as if we're waiting for someone to right a wrong, or waiting for anyone to right a past injustice in the present. We've given over the responsibility to someone else so we do not own our power to complete it. In this way, we begin to consider the realm of energy. Have you ever been around a person who is beaming, whose light you can see and feel? How does that feel inside you? Or the opposite, a person who fills their life with complaints and a way of talking that brings you down. Perhaps you never thought of it this way, but their energy is simply low and you feel it in their presence. By the choices you are making now, by the commitment to lead with courage and curiosity, you are choosing an energetic frequency. This frequency will have impact on what shows up in your life and who shows up in your life.

Fully living your experience is itself a process to engage with.

How can you do this in your marriage? Let your husband know your process, then invite him to join you in it, at least to the extent that you ask him to listen. You will assist him in supporting you by highlighting and simply bringing to the forefront of his attention that you want to live something differently. While this is for you, it will also create more intimacy, space, and love between you and your husband.

In this practice, you will be acknowledging what's been getting in the way. You may wish to do some writing about this or share with your husband the strategies you've been using up until now that you're coming to realize are no longer serving you.

I remember a time a few years ago when I came to understand that some of my friendships were based on a co-dependent way of operating as opposed to an interdependent one. I loved these women and I prided myself on supporting them and being the best friend I could be. What I didn't realize at the time was that I wasn't asking for what I needed, while I quietly maintained preconceived notions about how they "should" behave in response to my generosity. I was not a person who asked for help. I was not a person to seek the opinion of others. I was not a person who wanted to be perceived as needy. And I silently berated myself any time I became aware of feelings of disappointment when unspoken expectations were not met. After several years I came to realize that I wasn't satisfied in these relationships. I realized it was because I was not willing to be vulnerable. And when I started asking for their support and wanted the relationships to shift to better meet my needs, but I was still unwilling to be fully vulnerable, all three relationships ended.

What I learned from these relationships was that my own fear of intimacy and feeling out of control was getting in the way. At the time, I blamed them. But, in the following months, after reflection, pause, and inquiry, I came to understand myself as the common denominator. While I wished to grow in intimate relationship with them, I was closed off to that by not being vulnerable.

With the ending of those friendships and my lessons learned, other relationships began to show up. They were different and I was different. I started to ask for help. I risked vulnerability. I learned when to give support and when to listen versus needing to get in there and do something. My business practice changed, my primary relationship changed, and my relationships with my daughter and stepchildren changed. The practice of courage and curiosity brought me into deeper relationship.

EXERCISES

Rituals

One of my favorite sayings (especially with my family) is, "What was the missed opportunity?" This is also a reframing. We ask ourselves, "Are we operating out of love or something else?" One of the practices that creates more spaciousness and possibility for love in our home is the ritual of verbally and physically acknowledging each other: good morning, good night, hello, goodbye, kissing or hugging in the process. This was a practice I grew up with in my family, and if we didn't have this practice, I wonder if there would have been any intimacy between us. As I indoctrinated my husband and stepson into this practice, one that my daughter and I were already engaging in, the quality of our relationships as a blended family shifted. In the practice of hugging, I noticed the hugs grew in softness and length. There's a sold desire for connection now where there was once a sense of obligation.

We are formed by the rituals we choose to engage in.

When we miss an opportunity to practice this ritual, something feels off and there's a disconnection in my family. There's something easily misunderstood. I notice it quickly, and rather than focusing on what seems like the issue – two people not talking, or something being said or heard in the wrong way – I'll ask, "Did you hug this morning?" "Did you say good morning?" Nine times out of 10, they have not. Therein lies the gift and wisdom of the practice. It is the connection we are seeking. We will seek the connection one way or another. It's the reason why children have temper tantrums. It's the reason we hear, "Negative attention is still attention." Hmmmm...such good stuff to know that the underlying constant we are always seeking is to feel significant and to belong. We'll use strategies one way or another. This thinking turns everything on its head. Thus, creating your own rituals is an important practice in service to courage and curiosity.

Travel

On a recent trip overseas, I remembered why traveling is such an integral part of my life's journey. Visiting new lands and meeting new people submerges me in an aura of new perspective. In my experience, nothing has more impact on my self-perception and perception of the world, than traveling to a new place. Particularly, a new place where the culture, religion, or language is different than my own.

In this light, travel becomes a tool to open our eyes to new perspectives on the planet, different ways of living. Therefore, we cannot help but shift within ourselves. How can we judge another culture, religion, or language when we've lived among them even if only for a brief period? At a minimum, we get curious and recognize that we're more alike than we previously thought. The world feels a bit smaller, a bit less frightening, and we become a bit more loving in the process. If you're really ambitious, consider living in another country. Even one month will be a transformative experience. I realize that not all of us can jump on a plane anytime we're feeling the need to expand our horizons, myself included. Other ways to experience this shift would be reading and delving into new ideas from a variety of authors, or finding an environment to meet someone with a different point of view.

Creative Expression

I can remember when I was growing up that, as much as I enjoyed singing, it was not something my parents particularly valued. They acknowledged that it gave me pleasure, but in terms of taking it into my adult life, like many of us, it was not a skill that would make me money or one that I should consider exploring beyond a hobby, because I simply wasn't good enough. At least, that's how it felt. As I think back, I find it sad (and a missed opportunity!) that my creativity, voice, and other "non-quantifiable" qualities were categorized as such: 1) What would earn me money, and 2) What wouldn't. So, I focused on my studies and spent lots of time in class thinking, arguing, and debating. My brain was what I needed to develop so the attention that I could muster would go there, to the dismay of my creativity, my joy, and my passions. I kept singing "for fun" into my

20s and 30s, but it was in my 40s that I recognized the significance of developing this skill.

I had many teachers over the years, but one voice teacher stood out. When I met Daniel in 2011, I was ready to return to this love – my childhood passion – and see what it might bring forth. I never expected what would come – healing, such healing. Daniel helped me to journey with my breath, for example, into my back. Breathing in my back? Once there, I discovered a different sound, a different power. I sang to sing. I sang to cry. I sang to heal. I sang to remember and honor my parents, recording myself alongside a video I created and sharing the images and my voice with close family and friends at my mother's funeral. I sang to live. I sang to remember the little girl who played Dorothy in her 5th Grade school musical. I sang to remind myself of my innocence. I sang to open my heart. It's my observation that creative expression in the United States is highly underrated. It's perhaps become a normalized way of thinking that we wouldn't develop these skills as building blocks in our children. But I couldn't disagree more.

We are all creative human beings and, as such, it's our job to discover the best way to express that creativity and to keep that part of ourselves thriving. Sing, dance, draw, design, create! As you develop your relationship with your own creative self-expression, so too will you gain insight in the area of conflict. For example, if you're a visual artist, when you paint or draw, do you let it flow from you, or it is stop and go and stop, editing yourself along the way? As a vocal artist, every time I criticized my voice – particularly when I heard it recorded – I diminished my creative self-expression and fueled inner conflict. As we develop a loving relationship with our creative expression and all the challenges it may bring up for us, we are strengthening the very qualities that will support us in being with other areas of our lives where we struggle or are in conflict.

Curiosity and Courage

Becoming curious and letting go of assumptions allows other people to safely have their own experience with no belittling. Being present as a witness to someone's pain is more powerful than the most sentient advice. Allowing them time and space to grieve assists them to discover their own answers and know what they need.

When we can feel into the entirety of pain or disappointment, we actually open up the space for joy, connection and a new outlook.

CHAPTER 8

Dispelling the Big Lie: The Truth Won't Destroy Your World

"If you do not tell the truth about yourself
you cannot tell it about other people."
– VIRGINIA WOOLF

"I have learned now that while those who speak about one's
miseries usually hurt, those who keep silence hurt more."
– C. S. LEWIS

Children take everything literally. What parents tell their children feels like gospel truth, until it doesn't, and then our world is turned upside down. Like William Blake's *Songs of Innocence and Experience,* we woke up to a world requiring us to be cautious, if not savvy. How did this inform our experience of trust?

STEP 5: TRUST AND TRUTH TELLING

As children, we lived in this sweet place some-where in between curiosity and safety, only par-tially aware of our beingness, our presence, or the dangers that lurked. We looked to our parents and guardians to find our way. We trusted implicitly because we did not know any better. This was our reality. We took things literally, at face value. Our parents or guardians were our world, and through their eyes, through their lens, we came to know our own. While we believed we were seeing things with our own eyes, our parents were framing what we saw when they commented, judged, shared their opinions, and shared their world views. Their views were ever-present, informing what we took with us from our childhoods into adulthood.

One day, we each experienced the moment where there was a break. It was not a bad thing. It was simply a break from the innocence and sim-plicity, to being a little leery, a little hesitant, and a little more conscious of "the real world." Perhaps we were with our parents at the time, or maybe we were alone. It was a moment that we each held in our bodies, when curiosity and feeling com-pletely safe as little beings on planet Earth came to an end. We were initiated into another level of our human experience.

Consciousness of pain, separateness, and judgment – maybe we only felt it in our bodies, in our bones, but something was different. Enter trust. Who could we trust now? What do we trust? What is true and what is false? That feeling in my belly – what's that? The anger my father throws at my mother – what is that? The solitary feeling at school when I find myself alone on the playground, asking myself what I did wrong to be there – what is that? Trust – where does it come from?

More specifically, how do I know the difference between what I'm feeling, what seems true or natural, and what it is that my parents or other influencers around me tell me is true? What are my feelings and what are theirs?

These early childhood challenges formed the foundation for our adult challenges in relationship.

Authentic relationships exist to the extent that we are aware of the influences that have informed those relationships. For example, my father did not have consciousness around his anger. I don't remember him ever apologizing for his rage. I do not think this was intentional or that he meant to hurt us, but I also don't think he ever engaged in a process to understand where it came from. He never endeavored to grasp how to work with his anger so he could be released from it, so we could avoid the burden of bearing it and being told we were the cause of it.

Little by little, through the messages we received as children, the truth as we instinctively and intuitively knew it became less and less clear until we no longer understood the difference and could no longer reach within to know where to find the answers.

In my mid-20s, I remember participating in a workshop. There were about 80 people. The first exercise we did was called the "Trust Walk." In silence, we would walk around the room, look into the eyes of a stranger, and raise our right hand. One finger meant, "I trust you;" two fingers meant, "I don't trust you;" three fingers meant, "I don't know if I trust you;" and four fingers meant, "I don't care to say." My first thought was, "How can I know if I trust you if I've never met you or spoken to you?" I was very uncomfortable. I found my mind racing. Did I trust you because you looked nice, reliable, or trustworthy? Did I trust you because you were a man or a woman, or because you were older or younger, or because you looked like me, or because you were different? On and on. I must have met 40 people during that exercise, maybe more. Because I was so deep in my head trying to figure it out, and, frankly, get it right (surviving the exercise was the goal for me), I said, "one, two, three, four," in no particular order with no particular predictability. After the exercise, we were invited to consider our experience.

Remember, it's not through the experience that we learn, but by reflecting on the experience.

I was surprised by how uncomfortable I was during the exercise. I also noticed that I had a tendency to trust everyone. But, when this was questioned by the facilitator, I had to dig deeper into my motivations. Did I really trust everyone, or was I people pleasing and didn't want to hurt others' feelings, so I said I trusted them? This experience helped me become aware of how much discomfort I experienced with trust and truth-telling, and challenged me to begin the inquiry to understand why.

The step of trust and truth-telling, is the step to knowing what is true for you. In choosing to trust or not trust, you must tell the truth. Trust and truth-telling are therefore conjoined, and you can't have one without the other.

There are several reasons why you might find truth-telling difficult. First, for many of us, it was unsafe to tell our truth when we were children. If you came from a household where children were to be seen and not heard, then your parents were not interested in your truth. Second, many of us were raised by people who themselves did not know their own truth, so they could not mirror for us what our truth could look like or how to discover it. Third, we were conditioned out of our truth. When we did speak up and we were either denied or unrecognized, many of us received the message that our truth was wrong, unworthy, and insignificant. Then, we identified with that message. Truth-telling became a process by which we could be made wrong in some way. Truth-telling, though it represented our truest self, became a mechanism of our own undoing. Naturally, as children, we wanted the love, acceptance, and praise from our parents. At times, we may have denied our truth to get what we wanted.

By definition then, the very thing we are looking for in adult relationships – honesty, love, unconditional acceptance, the things we wanted as children – we could not get by telling our truth.

So many of us entered into adult relationships this way. No wonder there are so many unhappily married people. Using these same strategies to get into a relationship, we got a taste of safe vulnerability, and a taste of being seen, until we got the same message from our husband as we did from our parents. At some point it was no longer safe to tell our truth. There we were again, our 5-year-old self trying to get her parents attention to tell her truth. How ever we chose to do it, that part of us went back into hiding.

So, where do we go from here?

Surrender.

It wasn't your fault.

You didn't do anything wrong.

As you surrender into receiving this information through a new lens – one that understands that we, as well as generations before us, have repeated the same patterns and created the same misunderstandings, know that we now can surrender from making ourselves wrong or blaming someone else. Seek to understand, to see beyond the events and the thoughts about the events, and feel into the memories, into the truth of that moment. What felt aligned and what didn't? You can do this with your childhood and your current situation, but you must begin to surrender the stories about how it's been up until now and all the decisions you made about life. Choose to trust yourself and start telling yourself the truth, and then tell your husband, and then tell everyone else.

So many of us based our very existence – our safety – on living a lie, because we believed that if we told the truth our world would be destroyed. Having been in abusive relationships, including my relationship with my father, how many times did I consider saying what I really felt when I was being screamed at, threatened, or hit? Many times. Sometimes I did. Perhaps you can imagine that the repercussions in that moment were difficult to bear. The next time I would want to speak up, the prior consequences for speaking my truth informed me and caused me to hesitate. Who wants to rock their world? Who wants to anger their parent or spouse? Who wants to be told they are the cause of the anger or the conflict? Who wants to feel wrong or bad?

We suck it up for the sake of "peace." Ahhh! But isn't that the big lie? There is no peace in lying. There is no peace in not telling our truth. The short-term gain of avoiding conflict and discomfort becomes a high price to pay for long-term non-alignment, inner turmoil, and unhappiness. If you're paying that price, do you want to continue paying it?

Experiencing your experience – coming into a state where you can experience discomfort, conflict, and the resulting consequences – is valuable, although in the present moment it might not feel that way.

JUNE AND VICTOR

June deeply loved her husband – so much so, she would say she idolized him. She met him at a particular time in her life when she was dying inside for someone to see her. She wanted to live something bigger and experience something greater. She realized that her first marriage, while it taught her many things, was a bridge from childhood into adulthood. It showed her ways in which she was hiding. It gave her so many distractions, opportunities to take care of others, and excuses to not take care of herself, that it never really had a chance. So, when her second husband showed up in her life, she told herself what she needed to believe to make it OK to partner with him quickly after ending her first marriage.

But, without any time to reflect and learn from what she had been living in her first marriage (what she was avoiding, the excuses she was making, the fault she was doling out), things were no different with husband number two. New shiny man, same her. When they came to me, both in their second marriages, they were each on the verge of their second divorce.

The truth was, as much as she loved this man, they were on different paths with different priorities and core values. Being unaware of this at the beginning of their relationship meant they missed the yellow and red flags which surfaced early on in their courtship. They didn't know the right questions to ask and didn't follow their intuitions. They didn't ask themselves or each other why they had really left their former partners. They didn't dare address the similarities in their first and second partners. June's first husband was very much like her second and Victor's first wife was like June. They needed to keep the illusion that they were different from their previous spouses because this fallacy was keeping them together. The truth was that the patterns were not different, and the lessons they had not yet learned, remained.

Healing your relationships begins with learning to partner with yourself.

June, like many of us, was looking for a perfect relationship. She believed it existed outside of her.

But the perfect relationship, she eventually came to realize, was a relationship where she could tell her truth and her husband could tell his. In so doing, they were able to thoughtfully and lovingly heal many of their childhood wounds together, arrive at the conclusion that they were indeed on different paths, and divorce with love.

EXERCISES

Core Values Exercise

Our choices in life often reveal to us what our values are in any given moment. It's not hard to point out a family in a mansion with ten cars, a plane, and designer toilets and take a guess that they value luxury and comfort. What is more challenging is to sit down with ourselves and get honest about what our own lives reveal to us about what we value in this moment, particularly if we're experiencing inner conflict. This is when our external world does not reflect our inner desires.

I was introduced to a variety of exercises over the years that encouraged sitting, reflecting, and distinguishing my core values. The first time I did such an exercise, I was in my mid-twenties. When declaring my core values, I was actually making a statement about how I would like to live rather than how I was living at the moment. Since that time, at least once a year, I engage in some kind of exercise, workshop, or other practice where I sit with my core values. The practice is one of declaration and intention. I believe that what we declare at any given moment is what is most important to us. The question then becomes, "Are we willing to do, think, and feel what it takes to live that?"

Doing this exercise around New Year's Day can be a wonderful way to start the year. To do them with a friend, your spouse, and/or your children can be even more powerful. Becoming mindful of your core values and writing them down in a place you'll see them will assist you in knowing when you're on and off track. Here's my current list:

- Zen/peace
- Joy
- Simplicity
- Beauty
- Presence

My daily challenge is to check in with these core values and see when I'm on track and when I'm off. Soon after creating it, I already saw how it was supporting me in redirecting my attention toward the experience I wished to create and how I wanted to feel. It showed up in my physical home and office, family relationships, work relationships, client relationships, planning for the following year, and relationship with my body. This is a powerful tool, and one that can support you greatly.

When you first do this exercise, it might feel like you've finally discovered a hidden truth, a space inside yourself you've been hiding for a long time, maybe all your life. For others, it will be a first step to getting to know your truth and connecting with how you want to feel, what you desire, and what you've been holding back or pushing down for so long.

If you know your core values, what are they in this moment? Write them down and consider them. Do they reflect where you've been and where you're going? Any conflicts? Do they need some updating? If you've never consciously sat down and considered this, please find a core values exercise, and do this practice once a year. Many coaches and other practitioners have developed core values exercises and I use several in my mediation and coaching practice. Search "core values exercises" on Google and find one that works for you.

Water

It was incredibly amusing to me the day that I realized that my showers were, in fact, a meditation practice.

For years, I tried so many meditation techniques, and when I practiced them, they were great. They helped me clear my mind and get present. But often, when thoughts would enter, I resisted them because I was convinced that my mind was supposed to be empty. Gratefully, I found over the years that as I come into deeper alignment and practice with my purpose on the planet, my mind is less consumed with random thoughts and worries and is mostly still.

What I most longed for, however, was to hear more from "the little voice." The voice that is mine and, at the same time, not mine; the one that I know comes from "somewhere else;" the wisdom and guidance from the Universe, God, Spirit, angels, and so on.... Ten years ago, while taking a shower, upon hearing a message loud enough that I thought someone was in the shower with me, I understood two things. 1) It doesn't matter what we call it or where it comes from – I never need to debate or discuss the origin of that little voice for the rest of my life. All I need to do is follow it, because the messages are always in furtherance of my loving, self-expression, and passion. 2) The little (big!) voice often comes to me in water.

In telling many people about this experience over the years – how being in water has become akin to a meditative practice – I've heard others share similar experiences. We could trace the healing powers of water back to the beginning of time. Like breathing, we need water to exist. The practice here would be to discover the possible healing powers of water in your life.

Trust and Truth Telling

The confusion and distortion from our parents' untruths caused judgment and separation within ourselves. Have we modeled our own parents? How *could* we feel our own mate was 100% trustworthy if we couldn't trust parents to tell or know their own truth?

We have an inherent need for trust in relationships. To find it requires tools and practice. Is our "gut feeling" reliable? Meditation is one way to feel what is true and receive information from our deepest knowing. Seeking wisdom that allows you to feel connected with all that is provides solace and direction.

CHAPTER 9

Falling in Love with the Heartbreak

"In love, we bring each other fully into existence."
– RUMI

*"I will love the light because it shows me the way, yet I will
endure the darkness for it shows me the stars."*
– OG MANDINO

*"There is a sacredness in tears. They are not the mark of
weakness, but of power. They speak more eloquently than ten
thousand tongues. They are the messengers of overwhelming
grief, of deep contrition, and of unspeakable love."*
– WASHINGTON IRVING

We never forget our first romance. Mine was quick, with an exquisite soul, followed by deep sadness—alone again. Heartbreak allows us into the deepest recesses of our hearts, expanding it and letting us know just how profound and deep with meaning our lives can be.

STEP 6: INITIATION

No one ever forgets their first romance and their first heartbreak. I was 19. It happened during my first summer home from college. I had experienced dating and crushes, but never this. This was different: the kind of feeling one gets jumping out of an airplane (so I imagine), the thrill of the roller coaster for the first time, any first, I guess. I saw this man at a summer job and immediately my heart was in my knees. I'm certain I said to myself, "He'll never go for me. I'm too..." He had a girlfriend at the time. But when, in a turn of events, he broke up with this girl, he became interested in me. Being with him was like no other person I ever knew. He had charm, he was composed, and he had a mysterious air about him. Both of his parents had passed away when he was a child. I thought someone who experienced this kind of trauma at such a young age and radiated as he did must be pretty magnificent. He was my teacher, my lover, and my first heartbreak.

Our romance ended almost as quickly as it started. To my amazement and shock, I suffered. For three days, I cried and felt a pain and a heartache I did not known was possible. I was living with my father that summer, and he couldn't understand what had come over me. I didn't know what had come over me. I just knew such sweet sadness.

I was initiated into deep love and deep pain. As terrible as it felt, some part of me knew that it felt so terrible because that short-lived love affair felt so good. I had my first taste of love, of exchange with another, the exquisite feeling of longing for something and then get it. Then, its opposite: to have that something taken away, to be in the space without it, to not understand, to not have answers, and to feel so alone. At the time, I might have said it would have been easier never to have met him, never to have been in a relationship with him to avoid the pain. My authentic self knew differently. Certainly, as the years passed, I thought about him. But it wasn't really him I was thinking about – rather, it was the feeling I had in his presence. It was the feeling I had within myself of being wanted, connecting with another person so deeply, and even knowing that this kind of experience was possible.

The gift of heartbreak is to know the expanse of what your heart can and desires experience – the depth of love that we can experience on the planet. With that love comes heartbreak, because it is the other side of the coin.

We are here to experience it all.

The step of initiation is to recognize how both love and pain are gifts. Your heartbreak is a gift. It tells you how much you care and how important that person or situation was. If you didn't enjoy a job you were fired from, you probably wouldn't care. But get fired from a job you loved? You would be devastated. It's the same with love. Why do we fight so hard and long so deeply to stay in relationships way past their due date? Because we care, we want to understand, and we want to love and connect and feel both sides of the coin.

Many of us leave relationships before we've seen the whole picture. We certainly feel love at the beginning, and then on and off over a period of years – but more often we focus on the pain, disappointments, and unresolved arguments. We long for the deep connection, yet we focus on the lack, so we leave because we think we'll find it somewhere else. Much like those early heartbreaks, our marriages create many mini heartbreaks. But we generally don't leave our marriages after one big fight. We make love and re-connect, or spend a few days cooling off and getting some clarity, hoping this will be the last big fight. We look to those moments as the bad ones that we want to avoid.

But what if those mini heartbreaks, those conflicts, could be gifts that show you how much you care? How committed could you be to each other's happiness, to your own, if only the words and feelings didn't get in the way?

The belief that conflict is bad limits our access to love.

This step of initiation is one where you are presented with the possibility that your conflicts, heartbreaks, and disappointments are gifts to show you the depth and breadth of what you want to experience on the planet. When you begin to consider the lessons and opportunities your conflict is bringing you, then you can begin to fully embrace all the events of your life.

Your big, beautiful, complex, and sometimes complicated life.

Your experiences are no longer good or bad but simply experiences. This step then asks you, "How deeply do you want to feel? How fully do you want to live?" If you are like many – judging good and bad experiences, making yourself right and others wrong, particularly your spouse – then there is a limited range of experiences you can have in that paradigm. If you pause the judgment, and embrace the experience, what is it telling you? What is it asking you? What is it inviting you to consider next? What step does it want you to take?

The step of initiation invites you to expand your capacity to hold love and pain.

Falling in love with the heartbreak can undo us and help us grow. Here, we feel our capacity is greater than it was the day before it happened. How many times have we heard what doesn't kill us makes us stronger? It seems fitting here. Heartbreak does not literally break our hearts. When you feel into the pain, your heart expands, and you feel its presence. It's longing for you to know the capacity of your own heart. When our heart breaks for another, it reminds us of our capacity for empathy. We can feel what another is feeling because we've known that pain, even if the circumstances are different.

Empathy and compassion are more needed on the planet than ever before. If we choose to embrace our individual conflicts, we will have more capacity to sit in the presence of the conflicts around us and around the globe. From this place, we can influence the trajectory of the planet. If you're not interested in that, then imagine how increasing your capacity for compassion could impact your children and grandchildren? What is the legacy you wish to leave them?

EXERCISES

Nature

Being in nature – among the trees, the soil, water, wind and so on (forests and the ocean are my favorites) – gets us face-to-face with the synchronicity of life. Nature is constantly in conflict, in a sense. The existence of seasons means that four times a year, nature must bend and adapt to temperature and other climatic changes. It does so seamlessly and repeatedly. When I walk in the waves of the Pacific Ocean, the sand, rocks, and sea-dwelling creatures are tossed and turned in a continuous state of movement, shifting and adapting. Big waves will mean a certain behavior; smaller ones another behavior. Storms at the sea, low and high tide, the moon cycle, etc. – everything that lives in the sea responds. Nature can be our greatest teacher of how to be in flow with life, which includes how we respond to conflict and discomfort. As you're moving through your life, consider spending regular time in nature, as it assists you in coming into alignment with the entirety of your life's experience. Walk in the grass or the dirt, tend to a garden or plants, visit a forest, walk by the ocean, plant a tree, and consider nature's relationship to conflict as you explore your own.

Intention

How often do we move through life playing a role, doing our part, following someone's lead, and never stopping to ask ourselves, "What is my intention here?" "Where am I going?" "What's the point?" How often have I heard in sessions with divorcing couples that they never considered not marrying? They can remember falling in love and fostering that love for a time, but admit that many of the choices that followed came from an unconscious place – following what their parents, teachers, and community expected of them – rather than from a clear, intentional place. What a different relationship beginning it might have been to have the conversation early on around each person's intention for the relationship, intentions for the long-term, and goals for marrying or not. I often wonder (without regret for the choices I made), how I might have chosen differently if I had understood my intentions for how I wanted to live my life when I first married in my 20s, and then again in my 30s.

Ask yourself, "Am I living my life with intention? What is my five-year plan? 10-year plan? What are one or more values that guide me in my daily life? Consider how intention shows itself in your life and how you might use the power of your intention to move your life in the direction of your hopes and dreams.

Initiation

When we begin a relationship we wonder how long we'll be able to hang onto the love before the disappointments arrive—cherishing the good times, hoping not to be faced with "the bad."

But is it really bad? Could conflict be a way to gauge what you care about, what you'll fight for? Could conflict be a door to deeper love and understanding? By fully embracing it all, we foster gratitude for everything in our lives.

CHAPTER 10

Why I Love Conflict and Why You Should Too

"And so it is, that both the Devil and the angelic Spirit present us with objects of desire to awaken our power of choice."
- RUMI

This chapter focuses on the final countdown: making the choice to stay or go. As you reinforce your own desires, becoming mindful of what is not measuring up in your union and conscious about past misunderstandings, you will know how powerful this journey has been. The gift of choice is that you now have many more options in or out of your relationship than when you started this journey.

STEP 7: CHOICE

The first six steps of this process brought you to this moment to address the issue you were grappling with when you picked up this book: to make a choice.

If you've embraced the possibility of conflict as a gift, then the conflicts you had with your spouse may look very different now than they did yesterday or a few weeks ago. If those conflicts are helping you understand what is important to you, what was missing, what you've been longing for, as well as the misunderstandings you and your spouse were having, then you've arrived at a place where you can make a choice.

Your marriage and how you live it, is a choice. Do you choose to stay or go? Perhaps the more important question now is, how you will live that choice? Who do you want to be as you move through that choice? Knowing what you know now, what could be the benefits of staying or leaving?

Making a choice, and another and another, also makes way for completion. While many of us might be hesitant to choose, there is such joy in the choice because in choosing, there is freedom.

With choosing comes the responsibility to live out our choices. If your choice is divorce, I want to tell you that it's OK! If it's a choice to stay and start from scratch, even if everyone around you is telling you you're crazy, it's also OK!

When you live from an inner state of choice, there is true freedom as you shift from the perspective that "life happened to you" to "I make life happen for me." No longer a subtle victim, now you are a conscious chooser. Even if we don't always like the result of our choices – because we know there are no guarantees in life – how we interact with those results is a choice too!

How delightful!!!!!

From this mindset, you can experience the freedom to see conflict as an opportunity, as a lesson for your healing, as information, and as a gift.

I'll never forget watching the film "Life is Beautiful," which is set in an Italian concentration camp during World War II. It filled me with tears and laughter as the main character designed his world and experience in the concentration camp and shared it with those around him. He brought beauty, joy, and laughter in the most atrocious of situations. We could shrug this off and say it was just a movie, but have you ever met someone whose life seemed to be blessed? No matter what befell them, their attitude always seemed positive, or at least curious, as opposed to complaining, judging, and victimizing?

This is now your opportunity to step into your life as the decision-maker and co-creator. It's a chance to begin integrating everything you experienced into one big, beautiful package that is called your life. No longer must you look at events from the good/bad, right/wrong paradigm. Instead, you can see them all with a new set of eyes. You can inquire about, reflect on, and choose what interpretation suits you best today as you move forward towards the life you want to live. A life led by your principles, values, desires, and – if you know it – life purpose.

Are you loving the conflict yet?

Some would call me a masochist if I said I "liked" conflict. But loving conflict is different. For me, loving conflict is embracing it all. Loving conflict gives us the space to stop judging and shaming ourselves and others. It means we can break the chains of bondage that claim that there is one way to live out this human existence. It's time to start allowing all of us to have our own experiences, which simply means making space and allowing for the space between us as we live out our own truth. As a reminder, if you're judging someone else's truth or their life path, then there's probably something you're judging about your own. And judging theirs may be one more way you distract yourself from living out your own.

The choice to love conflict now means that you know where you are when you feel it: something's off, something needs to change, or something is not aligned. Conflict is your gift to let you know these things. It does not mean to go have a big fight, change someone else, or force your opinions on others. It does mean it's time to pause, breathe, consider, and reflect. It is here to serve you.

Choosing to love and embrace the conflict becomes a dance between you and conflict – not you and your husband, you and your boss, you and your children, or you and your parents – just you and conflict. How will you dance? How will you choose love within yourself when the conflict arises? How will you work within yourself to understand the deeper meaning and then have a conversation with the person who helped bring this forward for you (if that's even necessary) to move through it?

To love and embrace conflict means to consider a deeper truth. It reveals where the conflict resides. There, you'll find what may be the most difficult choice of all.

Your conflict resides within you. My conflict resides with me.

If conflict is a gift to each of us – information ultimately to help us individually become more

aligned with our own truth – then the job of working with conflict is entirely an inside job! The person with whom you are in conflict with suddenly
becomes inconsequential in terms of resolving
your inner conflict. When you choose to resolve
the conflict within yourself, you are free.

No longer will you need to have your point of
view agreed with. There appears now a deeper
understanding that can be shared. In this place,
the most magical things occur. From this place
of entirely owning, embracing, and resolving the
conflict within, your spouse is no longer responsible for your experience – you are. He is free to
have his own experience and do his own inquiry.
Whether he does will be up to him, but your experience will no longer be dependent on him doing
his work. You will feel at peace with him. When
you are the owner of your experience, he is able
to be the owner of his. Here is how we repair, acknowledge, forgive, and return to a loving state.

Ultimately, with this resolve, you will know
whether to stay or go. You will not wait for him to
make the decision for you, or for him to do something (or stop doing something) to convince you
to stay or force you to go. The choice is yours.

EXERCISES

Your Relationship Philosophy

Hopefully by now you understand much more about who you are, who your spouse is, and how you arrived at this moment in time. If you've done the practices, then they have led you to this moment of becoming a conscious co-creator of your life. Here's where creating your relationship philosophy comes in.

If we've been conditioned to enter into and live out our relationships according to the preferences of our families, religions, upbringings, etc., then our relationship experiences may not always have felt quite our own. We did not have a clear enough view of why we were entering a relationship to begin with. We learned about relationship from our families, but mostly likely no one ever sat us down to talk about the greatest possibilities in a relationship. Here's your opportunity to create that now, whether you choose to stay in or leave your marriage. As you clarify your relationship philosophy, it will send a vibrational signal to others who share your vision.

So much of the conflict we experience in relationship is simply a question of non-alignment, whether it be core values, purpose of relationship, or intention around what you wish to create or experience during your time on the planet. We've spent far too much time making each other wrong. When we have chosen marriage or a long-term committed partnership, it's even a harder truth to face. Alignment with our own relationship philosophy may shed light on the idea that it's time to go because the person with whom we are partnered has another path to follow. The old philosophy, "I'm unhappy and it's your fault," shifts to, "I understand the path that is mine to take, and you understand yours. As they are different paths, let's lovingly separate for us and our children."

Relationship Philosophy Process

If you look back to all the work you've done in the practices, you'll see all sorts of clues that were revealed through your words and thoughts: your core values, your relationship with conflict, and your prioritization of growth, evolution, healing, and repair as part of being in relationship. Did it resonate with you to say, "I am responsible for my experience" and to live by this? If so, that may be one of the first things you put in your relationship philosophy.

Here's an example:

- I choose to be responsible for how I experience all my experiences.
- My thoughts create my reality and inform my actions.
- Resentment, criticism, and guilt are the most damaging patterns that keep me stuck in my loneliness.
- I am loveable.
- I release the past and forgive everyone, as this is for my highest good, and they are simply a reflection of me.
- I am willing to sit with the question of what it means to love myself, and then learn to love myself and fall in love with myself again and again.
- When I really love myself, everything in my life works. This is when I can have interdependent relationships, when I can laugh at myself, and when I have complete freedom of expression.
- When I create harmony and balance in my mind and body, I find it in my life.
- Practicing unconditional love is the starting place, the place to live in, and the ending place. It is a state of being that exists within me.

- I have a path and certain experiences will repeat until I learn what I have come to learn from those experiences.
- I see my life from my point of view/my context. Moving into curiosity is the only path to truly seeing the other.
- Having any expectation that anyone was born to take care of me, or that everything in life should work exactly as I want, is setting myself up for suffering.
- My relationships are here to teach me many things, but the most important thing may be compassion – first for myself, then for others.
- It's not what's happening that is important. It's how I respond to what's happening.
- To live a whole life is to direct my attention regularly to my emotional life, mental/intellectual life, physical life, and spiritual life.
- Living from the context of 100% responsibility is a lifelong practice and may be the key to my capacity for unconditional loving.
- Every choice I am making is creating or denying a possibility for me and others to show up in authentic relationship.

Take your time with this and consider it well. Understand that, over time, your relationship philosophy may change as you evolve. You can only design your philosophy from where you are right now.

Find Your Tribe

As you live into this new way of being in your life, you might find that certain people no longer align with your outlook and what you wish to experience. They may fall away or leave abruptly. This is the time when you'll want to start seeking out your tribe. Writers like Seth Godin have used this language in recent years, and it's simply meant to help direct you towards people who share your philosophy. If your philosophy is aligned, at least in part, with what you've read in this book, then you likely won't be attracted to people who complain a lot; people who want to blame others; people who are right/wrong thinkers; people who are so set on one idea they don't have the patience or consideration to hear any other possibilities; and so on. Instead, your tribe may look like people who are seeking, people on a journey of inquiry – non-traditional medical practitioners, teachers, healers – people who use the word "life purpose" when they talk about their work, people who have an intentional attitude, and people who take personal responsibility in their lives.

Your tribe will play a great part in supporting you to continue on this path of inquiry, to live your life from the principles, values, and desires you articulate in your relationship philosophy, and manifest through your life purpose.

Choice

By examining your desires, you have opened the door to more freedom as a co- creator of your own life. How will you be a more enlightened partner if you decide stay? And who will you choose to be and what will you choose to live if you go?

Practicing "loving the conflict" means judgment or shame will have no voice in the process. Nothing about you or your partner is 100% bad or good, it just *is*. While both of you engage with the internal and external conflict, resolving your inner conflict will be the ultimate key to your freedom.

CHAPTER 11

A New Truth – Relationship as a Spiritual Practice

*"Some people awaken spiritually without ever
coming into contact with any meditation technique or
any spiritual teaching. They may awaken simply because
they can't stand the suffering anymore."*
– ECKHART TOLLE

"We don't see things as they are. We see things as we are."
– ANAIS NIN

We are here to express and discover who we are through our relationships. When we consider this as a "greater truth," then our relationships become a spiritual practice. Through this practice, I perceive what my soul is seeking to understand.

STEP 8: EXPLORATION

We didn't come here to prove something. We came here to be pure expressions of who we truly are.

As we come to the last step in "The P-R-A-C-T-I-C-E," we're now considering how we come to know ourselves through the eyes and the reflection of another. It's time to take things one step further. I suggest that our relationships also present us with the ability to know the Universe, Spirit, God, and our Oneness, and as such, relationships are a spiritual practice.

In my experience, attending religious schools and taking part in religious traditions throughout my childhood did not help me to answer the deeper questions. Why am I here? What's my purpose? What's this all about? At the age of 12, when I read *Are You There God? It's Me, Margaret* (thank you Judy Blume), I became angry at the idea that this girl, no older or wiser or more special than me, had a direct relationship with God through her journal. That moment was my initiation into "the inquiry" and the questions that would haunt me and delight me for decades to come.

I continued questioning into my 20s and 30s, searching, seeking, and struggling more than having that direct relationship with "something bigger than myself." It would only be in my early 40s, a time of awakening for many people, when I heard the words of the French philosopher Pierre Teilhard de Chardin and everything shifted for me.

You are a soul having a human experience.

Through my teachers Ron and Mary Hulnick, I also heard it as, "You are a soul *using* a human experience."

How curious! How amazing! No longer was I searching for the soul or my purpose. I was a soul! The core of who I was, my very essence, was my soul. Suddenly I recognized that the body I occupied, the family I came from, and the skills I had developed along the way, were not the whole story. Not even close. The story I was now interested in was the journey of my soul, and what my soul was trying to understand through these human experiences. More specifically, through conflict, change and transition.

The idea that my life up to this "awakening moment" was only a tiny version of what was possible, scared me. Yet, it excited me too! After more than 30 years of questioning, challenging, contradicting, and fighting, I was given the gift of reorganizing my worldview. This led to an expansion of what I could now feel, understand, and experience, as a soul having a human experience.

JOHN AND SUSAN

John and Susan came to me because they were having communication issues. They had been together thirty years. While misunderstandings and hurts had piled up over the years, there was also a lot of great love lived. They shared intimately about their desire for each other and their struggles – emotional, physical, and otherwise. As I listened to them and admired their courage and willingness to be so revealing and vulnerable, John shared how he had not had a formal occupation since his 40s due to work-related injuries. In rapid succession, Susan shared how John spent much of his waking life repeating stories from the past, 50-year-old stories that she had heard more times than she could count.

As I continued to listen and ask questions, it occurred to me that this was not a communication issue. Many of us struggling in a relationship often think communication is the issue. What I heard was something else.

When John opened up about his past (with his patient wife listening to the stories yet again), he shared that he had a rich and vibrant career in publishing industry, the armed forces, and several other industries. In the prime of his life – when twenty-five years of rich personal and professional experience could have translated to positions of authority and being sought out as a thought leader – he was injured. Coincidentally, this was the time when John and Susan met, and soon thereafter married. At the prime of their relationship, John was at an all-time low in his career and his "standing" in the world.

When I shared this observation with them, their eyes blazed as they came to have a new understanding of the great struggle of their relationship. This was not a communication issue; this was a life purpose issue. While Susan had continued to thrive in her career and artistic endeavors during their marriage, John did everything he could to keep busy (including creating conflict as a distraction) and ignore the fact that somewhere inside he had felt aimless and insignificant for decades. As we discussed the idea of life purpose – of tapping into something bigger than our physical, emotional, and mental experiences – the tension and fear that had been brewing between them began to dissipate. The upset feelings they had blamed on each other began to dissolve. Together, we went on to have a very different kind of conversation.

How would your life feel if you were to experience it through a spiritual context?

SARAH AND MICHAEL

Sarah and Michael had been struggling to stay together when they reached out to me. While very much in love, Sarah felt she and Michael were not on the same page. She wanted him to "meet her where she was." As hard as Michael tried, he couldn't figure out what that meant and any effort to do so, fell flat. As a result, they had been on the verge of ending their 6-year relationship numerous times.

Sarah decided to take some space and travel alone to visit family overseas. One evening, a few days after she returned, Michael was in the kitchen preparing dinner. Sarah was lying on the couch still recovering from jet lag. They were talking and reconnecting. Michael had become much more communicative over the years, and he was sharing his feelings about Sarah, how he missed her when she was gone, and how he had understood some things during her absence.

Suddenly, out of nowhere, Sarah said, "I don't believe that God or the Universe or whatever it is that's out there has my back or really gets me." She thought it was such a strange thing to say out loud, and yet, it struck at something deep inside of her. She started to sob.

What did it mean? As she sat with her emotions and the swelling heaviness in her chest, she felt a big revelation move through her body. She said, "If I don't believe that God or the Universe or whatever we call it has my back or really gets me, how could any human being have my back or really get me?

She looked at Michael and, with tears in her eyes, said, "You never had a chance."

It was in that moment that she realized that every relationship in her life had been doomed.

She lived with the underlying, unconscious belief that it was impossible to be known, cared for, and for someone to have her back. Sarah couldn't determine where this belief came from, but, in that moment, it didn't matter. What mattered was that, in realizing this she could mentally and emotionally "free" every person she had been angry with, or disappointed by, or resentful of. For the first time, she could see so clearly how her unconscious beliefs had disallowed the very experiences she longed for.

This was her initiation into a new kind of love, a new kind of opening, a new kind of willingness, and a new possibility for committed relationship.

Sarah and Michael married two years later.

No more fear of the "woo woo." No indoctrination. Just questions, and questions that beget questions.

This is what it means to experience your life through the spiritual context. From this place, you will see your experience as your own. You will live it out fully through the eyes of your soul. You will be diligent in coming to understand the experiences – the lessons, the healing, and the love – that your soul is seeking to know.

EXERCISES

Inquiry

As a child raised in the Jewish tradition, there is one piece of wisdom that has always stuck with me. When I spent time in Israel just after my father's passing, I attended a lecture with a well-known Rabbi. He was explaining his controversial statements regarding the personal responsibility of Jews during the Holocaust. I was both shocked and intrigued that someone who was so steeped in this religion, whose own family had been killed at the hands of the Nazis, and who lived in a country surrounded by people who could alienate and expel him for such statements, was talking about personal responsibility of people who, by all accounts, were victims of horrible crimes. As he continued and referenced teachings in the Bible, what I heard was that Judaism is a religion based on the ability to be in a question. We ask questions. When we're done with one question, we go on to the next. In a room of young men and women at a pivotal time in our development (I myself was in the middle of an identity crisis, torn between two phases in life, two religions, the death of my father, and the departure of my mother as she returned to her country of origin), his words could not have been more relevant and necessary. I left that seminar still seeking answers as my heart and intuition reminded me that the learning, guidance, and wisdom would be found in the question.

When I work with clients today or sit with my daughter as she struggles through a conflict with a friend, it's the Rabbi's invitation that I consider. I ask questions: "What is it about this situation you're most conflicted about?" "What do you think she meant by that?" "What part of you is hurt by her words?" Being in an inquiry is not simply about asking questions.

It's an orientation to life.

It is built on the premise that you are curious about life rather than judging, assessing, and putting it into categories. With that curiosity, you are seeking to learn, understand, build on your personal experience, and touch into your authentic knowing. The inquiry invites opening and possibility. The inquiry is inviting.

Here's the practice. Take one situation in your life right now and get into an inquiry about it. Notice what it feels like to move out of judgment or right/wrong thinking and move into the question. Have I been here before? If so, what's similar? What's different? What am I feeling? Where in my body am I feeling it? What do I want to say? What feels true to me in this moment? If I'm in judgment about him/her/them/it, then what could be underneath that?

Visioning

What is next for you? It's an exciting moment. Everything is possible. If you're choosing to remain in your marriage, it may feel like you're starting from scratch, because your partner looks different through your "new eyes." Now your mind and heart are open to new possibilities. What does that say about this process? Remember, and I cannot stress this enough, it's an inside job.

After many years of observing couples who separate, I think the lack of clarity around the joint "big picture" trumps the money, time, kids, lack of sex/intimacy, and other reasons people state for the end of the relationships. What is a relationship, after all, but a commitment to something bigger than the contribution, creation, and manifestation you could create on your own?

1 + 1 = 3!

I believe that working from the premise that a relationship is a spiritual practice infers that something greater is possible when two people come together – greater than what either of them could do on their own. 1+1 does not simply equal 2. 1+1=3!

There are many ways to get to that vision, and how you do your visioning may look different over time. You can do vision boards, you can write, you can create an ideal scene: your ideal day, week, month, or year. There are many ways to tap into a vision you now wish to step into. Consider creating a personal vision board and then one with your spouse. Or simply start a "Life List" where you write down experiences you wish to have.

Music

Music brings joy. All around the globe – in every culture, country, and language – music connects us to ourselves, each other, and to Source, Spirit, God, and the Oneness. In my personal practice, I have found that no other way tops this one to get me into my emotional body and out of my head. Music gets me up and moving, vibrating on a higher frequency. It can bring me to my knees into melancholic Oneness with my pain and the pain of the world. It's why we love the videos we see of spontaneous outbursts of song and music on the Internet. We watch in part for the music and musicians, dancers, and performers, and we also watch for reactions from the audience. As they are moved, so are we. We are unified.

Holding Space for Another and Witnessing

Holding space for another and witnessing, is a state of being. It embodies "The P-R-A-C-T-I-C-E." It means having the willingness to sit with another person in deep listening, deep witnessing, and sharing from the place of personal responsibility and love. By the practice of holding space for others, you will provide opportunities for them to do so as well. You have the tools now.

On a final note, I thought of titling this book, "Your Hardest Relationships Are Your Greatest Teachers," but didn't think that would be very appealing. Now that you're nearing the end, let's talk about this concept.

Among my most difficult relationships, my father comes first. Parents are the difficult relationships that keep on giving.... Even 28 years after his death, I am still regularly confronted with memories of the challenges, hurts, and misunderstandings between us. I see him in some of my relationships today. I see him in myself. I think of him every day when I look at a picture of us on my mantle, me in his arms at the age of one. He is very present with me. He is my teacher, perhaps my greatest teacher. He's still teaching me. From this perspective, I want the thoughts and feelings to come, I want to understand, and I am receptive to learning. I no longer take the viewpoint of "getting over it," and moving on so I can get on with my life. Those thoughts feel so foreign now, yet once they were the only thoughts I had of him... along with many much more negative ones.

I won't ever know what his soul was seeking, I won't ever know what it was like for his human experience. But it is my willingness to continue acknowledging that I am in relationship with him and learning from him every day, just like my two ex-husbands, my mother (who also passed), and the people who come in and out of my consciousness from many years ago. I am, in some ways, in as much relationship with them as I am with the family I live with, the clients I work with, and the community of which I am a part.

Our past relationships are not as in the past as we might think. They can continue to be our greatest teachers. The difficult ones remind us that there are things we're still figuring out and things our soul is still exploring in our human experience. Our other relationships remind us of the love, gratitude, and simplicity that can exist in unconditional loving. The difficult relationships remind us of this too, once we embrace the idea that they are our teachers.

Exploration

Inquiry is a way to find what you know within yourself. My heart and my intuition reminded me that learning, guidance, and wisdom could be found *in the questions we ask, not necessarily in the answers.* To remember who you really are:

1. Begin with the premise that you are *curious about life* rather than judging.

2. Work with visioning to see your partner through "new eyes," and create new possibilities

3. Embrace music and song as tools to change your frequency, shake negative emotions, and get you out of your head and into your heart.

4. Hold space for another person in deep listening and witnessing.

5. Remember that your most difficult relationship may be your greatest teacher.

CHAPTER 12

Integration

*"It's a helluva start, being able to recognize
what makes you happy."*
- LUCILLE BALL

When we learn something mentally, we must then transition the knowing to our bodies to fully integrate the learning. That is the journey – your journey – the period of days, weeks, or months it took you to read this book and the life you've lived in the interim. By now, you know the right answer for you, though the "how" of how it's all going to play out is most certainly not 100% clear.

How will you live this next chapter? How will you ensure that you live your answer well? No matter what you have chosen – to reignite your marriage or to separate with love – how well you will live either of these paths is based on how willing you are to integrate what you have learned from the practices.

Now to address an uncomfortable question: what would keep you from doing this work? Living as your highest self, and truth-telling when unwanted consequences might be at hand is not easy. So much of what you discovered is based on just that. You lived your life up until now avoiding discomfort and conflict whenever possible (even if you're a fighter), and that strategy served you well in maintaining some state of comfort, even if it meant you weren't getting the life you wanted.

Now I'm telling you that, to get what you want, you will have to address your discomfort and face the conflict before you. Not the conflict you thought was the issue, rather, the conflict(s) within *you* that you're now willing to bring forward. Some would argue that life is not supposed to be uncomfortable. I think now you understand otherwise. It's time to dive into the discomfort, in little bits at a time – whatever you can handle – and sit with it until you're through to the other side. It may be for just a few moments or it may be longer. For me, I have lived through many dark nights and they still come around, but I no longer resist them. I now know that by doing the practices and allowing time for integration, there is so much joy, clarity, and freedom on the other side. And the dark nights are a part of that journey.

I always loved daydreaming and thinking big. I could imagine so many glorious possibilities for my life. That was never the scary part for me. The scary part was how to carry them out, facing what would be asked of me to live out those dreams: to find my voice, speak my truth, and face potential naysayers. In doing so, facing my fears.

What is the cost of not doing the work? If you think back to when you first picked up this book – when you heard about another possibility of how to live your divorce or revitalize your marriage – consider the thoughts and feelings you had about your life: the powerlessness, discouragement, fear, sadness, frustration, and anger. How long were you living this way? This is the cost of not doing the work. It's your joy, freedom, and desires that fall by the wayside. It's another month, year, or decade gone, longing for the life you know you could have but are afraid to *live*.

While you may think that doing the work is hard, there are many practices within these pages that simply invite you to notice your world a bit differently and consider another possibility. There are no hard and fast doctrines, or right or wrong ways of doing it. In fact, I believe "The P-R-A-C-T-I-C-E" is simply a roadmap to finding your own way.

Make this your own. Do it at your own pace. Then do it over and over and over again until you feel it's time to practice something else.

Most importantly, if there's one practice that far outweighs the rest, ask open-ended questions. Ask questions of yourself, your loved ones, Source, Spirit, God, your colleagues, your parents, and your children. Put a question mark on half of the sentences you speak, and your life will be transformed. In a question, there is pause. In a question, there is space. In a question, there is a desire to know. In a question, there is an invitation. In a question, there is humility. In a question, there is curiosity. In a question, there is courage to face an unknown answer and unknown experience. In a question, we reveal what we don't know. In a question, there is humility. All that is in a question.

As you move through your life becoming masterful in your questioning, your truth and the truth of others will be revealed. You will notice you grow slightly more and more comfortable in the not knowing, in the pause, and in the space that exists between you and another, and you and your source. You will begin to revel in that space, because that questioning space invites wisdom, truth, intuition, and higher guidance.

You – as a soul, having a personally responsible, accountable, truth-telling, and courageous human experience – are now the co-creator of your life with your husband, your partner, your children, your parents, yourself, and your source. You now have the wisdom and insight to design your life as you would have it be.

You will be that space for yourself – the source of your own happiness, of your own beautifully designed life, of the love you desire, and of all the relationships you will co-create.

Integration

To get what we want in life, we must address discomfort and face the conflict.

The irony of a life well-lived is that it's uncomfortable. And, by doing the practices and allowing for time to integrate, there is so much joy, clarity and freedom on the other side. Discomfort and joy. Conflict and freedom.

CONCLUSION

You've been on a beautiful and difficult journey. By now, it's my hope that you have found your own answers from deep within yourself: truths that you can call your own and use as guideposts as you move forward in your messy, beautiful, complicated, and wonderful life. It's my dearest wish that, as you move forward, you will remember it's OK to have more questions than answers. It's OK to not know what you don't know – even better, not knowing invites greater wisdom and a greater human experience for your soul.

You have power now because you understand that you have choices. You can choose to live your commitment and see your difficulties as opportunities. You can continue to do your own personal growth work and explore every corner available to you. You understand now that there are other layers of your life that you were once unaware of, and that these layers are available for you to live a bigger life than you have lived up until now. This is real power. It's the power to choose something bigger and more profound, to be with your experience and the experience of others, and to slowly learn and embody acceptance.

I want to remind you that conflict is here for your soul's growth. I don't know what your life experience has been but I am empathic. Remember that the difficulties are here for you, not against you. If you continue to ask the questions of what they are here to teach you, you will find big, beautiful answers, and it will make sense. Remember the pause and the patience, because many answers do not come forward quickly, but rather, in their own time, and when you are ready to receive them.

I want to remind you to remain curious on your path. Hardened opinions, statements, and judgments will bring you more difficulty and confusion. Staying curious means asking the questions, but more so having a mind that is open to answers and experiences of others, particularly when they do not mesh with your own. This is not easy, dear reader, and I do not want to imply that it is. I stand with you as I continue to live my own questions and heal my own wounds that continue to reveal more layers. The little voice in the back of my head reminds me that this is *for* me and not against me. Rather than trying to run from the sadness or sit in judgment, I ask for guidance. I sit in the wonder and the sadness, and slowly, the truth comes forward. This is "The P-R-A-C-T-I-C-E."

I want to remind you to examine your expectations. My mother always told me expecting things was bad and would only bring me displeasure. Instead, I ask of you, where do your expectations come from? Are they yours or another's? Do these expectations still serve you? Are they getting you what you want? Is it time to let go of them and create commitments and new agreements from the place you are standing in now? How might that feel differently?

If you're in the boat of still hoping that your husband will show up differently, I'm sorry to say, there is no hope there. As Gandhi said, "It's time for you to be the change you seek in the world." Examining your expectations will be a delicate inquiry with yourself, of the life you thought you would have, and the one you are in now. Be loving and patient with yourself as you go through this process. You are designing your life.

I want to remind you to be responsible for your experience. I believe this is key, as I come back to this one every day with clients and with myself. Remember that being responsible for your experience doesn't mean you made them do it, or that you're responsible for everything bad in the world. What it means is that you can rise to the occasion and you have choice in how you receive the other person in front of you, in what you say about them, what you think about them, and in what you will choose to believe going forward from that situation. Being responsible for your experience also means that you get to experience it. In doing the practices, you will learn to be more present in this moment so that you can really live it without the anxiety and desire to run from it when it's uncomfortable. Because it will get uncomfortable. Our human experiences are designed that way!! When you remember this, you will feel a little less resistant, a little less angry, and a little less frustrated. Your experience of the experience will transform as you seek the lesson within it.

I want to remind you, dear reader, that resolving your relationship conflicts is not optional. If you walk away from your relationship, it may be the perfect choice for you and the right thing to do, but whatever internal conflict you are experiencing regarding your relationship will continue to rest unresolved within you until you do the work to resolve it. However you approach this, believing that simply not being with your husband is the answer, is not the answer. This is because the conflict never resided in him. The conflict will remain if we do not address it within. The form might look different (different guy, same experience), but everywhere we go, there we are.

I want to remind you to allow yourself to be seen through the eyes of another. How many times did I want to force someone to see me, only to be reminded that it's in my most vulnerable and willing moments of surrender that I am most seen. It is your work to get there, not someone else's. In allowing yourself to be seen, you take responsibility for your experience, wishes, and desires. When you focus on what you want to experience and what you want them to see, and you show them, they see you. They want to see you! Remember to have the courage to be vulnerable and be seen.

Most of all, dear reader, I want to remind you that today is practice for tomorrow. There is no place to "get to" or perfection to be reached. It is in the living today and the small steps that we will know: correct action, words, and thoughts. Today, as a practice for tomorrow, reminds us to soften in how we walk today and create spaciousness when we make a "mistake" or when we say or do something we wish we hadn't. Keeping in mind that repair is available all the time and it too is a gift. In our relationships, when we say or do something we regret, it's a beautiful opportunity to make amends, repair hurts and misunderstandings, and build our capacity to operate from love.

Here's to many more beautiful opportunities to operate from love.

ACKNOWLEDGEMENTS

My mother always said, "Nothing of value happens overnight." Never was this truer for me than in the process of writing this book. While I often criticized myself during the process, I was lucky enough to have people surrounding me, cheering me on, and reminding me to be gentle with myself (and not forget to laugh). Most importantly, they encouraged me to complete. For them, I am eternally grateful.

To Angela Lauria and The Author Incubator team, who helped me bring this process to completion in a swift, professional and divine manner.

To my beloved teachers, mentors, and coaches, who guided me with courage and grace: Bettie Spruill, Isis Fuqua, Ray Blanchard, Charlene Afermow, Lauren MacNeill, Renee Spears, Brian Whetten, Nicole Whetten, Ron Hulnick, Mary Hulnick, Daniel Buchanan, Lawrence Conlan, Surinder Singh, Jorge Haddock, Lisa Kalmin, Chris Lee, and Terry Nelson.

To my tribe, brainstorming partners, soul siblings, and tireless readers of my work: Madeleine Eno, Jennifer Savage, Petra Nicoll, Scarlett Mosier, Kathy Carlisle, Diane Plessia, Luc Dubay, Vinciane Lefevre, Jackie Adler-Tripicco, Melissa Rivera, Anna Chapman, Ruth Brennan, Michelle Anita Wirta, Judy Schiller, Adrienne Hays, Monica Tyson, Michael Breault, Jane Kronick, Meredith Mani, Mahadeva Mani, Bryn Johnson, Kathy Hedrick, Kiran Rapal, Jacqueline Seas, Aerin Alexander, Linda Cohen, Jennifer Paauwe-Riffe, Wren Shiffler, Jennifer Jacoby, Bertrand Lauret, Sharon Ann Rose, Christy Christopher, Joanna Mastalerek, Frank Marion, Walter Werzowa, Stu Bone, Matthew Carlson, Alejandra Brockmann, Carole Downing, Katherine Friedman, Joshua Edwards, and Kristin Ford and Rosemary Sneeringer.

To my clients, who trusted me with the most intimate details of their lives, and inspired me with their courage.

To my family, who challenged me, loved me, cheered me on, and held my feet to the fire, reminding me to practice what I preach: Blair Barnes, Siena Causevic, Bram Barnes, Elvir Causevic, Loren Causevic, Vivian Causevic, Miriam Zylberman, Claude Katz, Marilyn Vore, Martine

Harris, Rick Harris, Joel Harris, Marc Harris, and Tran Harris.

And to my parents who instilled in me the challenges, the questions, and the gifts: Colette Dawance and David Zylberman.

THANK YOU

Now that you've finished reading this book, you are on the path to discovering what is next for you in your relationship. In continued support and commitment to your success on this journey, please visit www.theradicalapproach. com for a free class that you can take today to support you in continuing the inquiry with me.

I wish you so much love and joy.

ABOUT THE AUTHOR

B elinda Zylberman, JD, MA, is a transformative mediator, relationship coach, and "spiritual psychology" who has guided hundreds of women and men through their most difficult relationship conflicts for over ten years.

Her mission is to transform the paradigm of conflict by challenging couples to consider the healing and lessons that lie within their most difficult moments. She firmly stands by the philosophy that "our most difficult relationships are our greatest teachers."

Through her business practice, Paikea Mediation, Ms. Zylberman combines skills and education gained from her studies and practice of law, mediation, spiritual psychology, anthropology, and communication, to support people to find compassion and healing on the other side of conflict. She's traveled to over 50 countries and loves witnessing the unique and not-so-unique ways people fight and love all around the world.

She believes that, by engaging in a process through which we can decipher and absorb the lessons that lie beneath conflict, we are inevitably led to our most sought out human experience, love. This means not simply resolving conflict, but healing through the practices of deep listening and being with conflict.

In a time when polarization and conflict are rampant, Belinda's philosophy – that we're all on this journey together and the person we may have deemed our enemy can be our greatest advocate – is sorely needed. Belinda is an author, speaker, and humanist. She co-authored the Amazon bestseller Putting Kids First in Divorce: How to Reduce Conflict, Preserve Relationships and Protect Children During and After Divorce.

Belinda currently lives in Portland, Oregon, with her husband, daughter, and stepson, and plans to take her "show on the road" in the next few years, bringing her philosophy, passion, and commitment to national and international platforms.

Find out more about Belinda:

Website: www.paikeamediation.com

Email: Belinda@paikeamediation.com

Linked in: www.linkedin.com/in/belindazylberman

DIFFERENCE
P R E S S

ABOUT DIFFERENCE PRESS

Difference Press is the exclusive publishing arm of The Author Incubator, an educational company for entrepreneurs – including life coaches, healers, consultants, and community leaders – looking for a comprehensive solution to get their books written, published, and promoted. Its founder, Dr. Angela Lauria, has been bringing to life the literary ventures of hundreds of authors-in-transformation since 1994.

A boutique-style self-publishing service for clients of The Author Incubator, Difference Press boasts a fair and easy-to-understand profit structure, low-priced author copies, and author-friendly contract terms. Most importantly, all of our #incubatedauthors maintain ownership of their copyright at all times.

LET'S START A MOVEMENT WITH YOUR MESSAGE

In a market where hundreds of thousands of books are published every year and are never heard from again, The Author Incubator is different. Not only do all Difference Press books reach Amazon bestseller status, but all of our authors are actively changing lives and making a difference.

Since launching in 2013, we've served over 500 authors who came to us with an idea for a book and were able to write it and get it self-published in less than 6 months. In addition, more than 100 of those books were picked up by traditional publishers and are now available in book stores. We do this by selecting the highest quality and highest potential applicants for our future programs.

Our program doesn't only teach you how to write a book – our team of coaches, developmental editors, copy editors, art directors, and marketing experts incubate you from having a book idea to being a published, bestselling author, ensuring that the book you create can actually make a difference in the world. Then we give you the training you need to use your book to make the difference in the world, or to create a business out of serving your readers.

ARE YOU READY TO MAKE A DIFFERENCE?

You've seen other people make a difference with a book. Now it's your turn. If you are ready to stop watching and start taking massive action, go to http://theauthorincubator.com/apply/.

"Yes, I'm ready!"

DIFFERENCE
P R E S S

OTHER BOOKS BY DIFFERENCE PRESS

Am I The Reason I'm Not Getting Pregnant?: The Fearlessly Fertile Method For Clearing The Blocks Between You And Your Baby by Rosanne Austin

Career or Fibromyalgia, Do I Have To Choose?: The Practical Approach to Managing Symptoms And The Life You Love by Karen R. Brinklow

Damsel No More!: The Secret To Slaying Your Anxiety And Loving Again After An Abusive Relationship by Emily Davis

Help! My Husband Is Hardly Home: 8 Steps to Feel Supported While Raising Your Family by Kelsey Domiana

The Divorced Mom Makeover: Rise Up, Reclaim Your Life, And Rock on With Your Gorgeous Self by Jamie Hernandez

The Right Franchise for You: Escape the 9 To 5, Generate Wealth, & Live Life on Your Terms by Faizun Kamal

Overcome Thyroid Symptoms & Love Your Life: The Personal Guide to Renewal & Re-Calibration by Vannette Keast

The Luminary Journey: Lessons from a Volcano in Creating a Healing Center and Becoming the Leader You Were Born to Be by Darshan Mendoza

The End Is Near: Planning the Life You Want After the Kids Are Gone by Amie Eyre Newhouse

When Marriage Needs an Answer: The Decision to Fix Your Struggling Marriage or Leave Without Regret by Sharon Pope

Leadership Through Trust & Collaboration: Practical Tools for Today's Results-Driven Leader by Jill Ratliff

Conquer Foot Pain: The Art of Eliminating Pain by Improving Posture so You Can Exercise Again by Julie Renae Smith

The Art of Connected Leadership: The Manager's Guide for Keeping Rock Stars and Building Powerhouse Teams by Lyndsay K.R. Toensing

Financial Freedom for Six-Figure Entrepreneurs: Lower Taxes, Build Wealth, Create Your Best Life by Jennifer Vavricka

Begin Again Differently: 7 Smart Processes to Win Again after Suffering a Business Loss by Claudette Yarbrough

The Joy of Letting Go of Your Biomedical Career: The Ultimate Quitter's Guide to Flourish Without the Burnout by Xuemei Zhong